CRY
OF THE
HEART

LORENZO ALBACETE

foreword by CARDINAL SEÁN O'MALLEY

CRY
OF THE
HEART

On the Meaning of Suffering

CRY OF THE HEART
On the Meaning of Suffering

Slant Books
P.O. Box 60295
Seattle, WA 98160

www.slantbooks.com

Cataloguing-in-Publication data:

Names: Albacete, Lorenzo | O'Malley, Cardinal Seán

Title: Cry of the heart : on the meaning of suffering / Lorenzo
Albacete

Description: Seattle, WA: Slant Books, 2023

Identifiers: ISBN 978-1-63982-127-3 (hardcover) |ISBN 978-1-63982-
126-6 (paperback) | ISBN 978-1-63982-128-0 (ebook)

Subjects: LCSH: Suffering | Suffering--Religious aspects | Suffering of
God

Contents

Foreword

TOWARDS THE END OF her life, Doña Conchita Cintron Viuda de Albacete lay almost motionless in her nursing home bed. She was a shadow of her former self, and she looked so tiny that she could have been an injured bird that fell from the nest and was tucked carefully into the covers. The twinkle in her eyes was gone, her riotous sense of humor evaporated along with her beautiful smile, her winsome personality, and her incredible *don de gente* (people skills). I remember visiting her in the nursing home and seeing her curled up in the bedclothes. It was heart-rending.

I took her hand and called her by name, but she no longer recognized me or had the strength to respond. Then I noticed the huge portrait of the Sacred Heart of Jesus that her son Lorenzo had placed directly over his mother's bed. I knew it was Lorenzo who had put it there because below the picture in very large print was written: "¡APESAR DE TODO, GRACIAS, SEÑOR!" (In spite of everything, thank you, Lord).

The phrase was vintage Lorenzo, not just because it was zany, but because it said something profound in the midst of humor. St. Francis used to say that the cross was his book. Lorenzo spent a lot of time studying that book where he discovered so much about the first Adam and the second Adam — the first whose disobedience brought death into the world and the second whose obedience brought grace and new life. The tree of the garden of Eden is replaced by the tree of the cross.

For many people, science, technology, and medicine have replaced faith as the compass for their lives. We live in a world of secularization, political correctness, cancel culture, and strident polarization. One author has described the Church as a colony of resident aliens. St. Paul says that our commonwealth is in heaven and Lorenzo would use that to show that we are a colony of heaven. Like the Jews in the diaspora, believers are strangers in a strange land. A colony is an outpost, a beachhead, an island of one culture in the middle of another, a place where the values of the homeland are passed on to the young, the place where the distinctive language and lifestyle of resident aliens are lovingly nurtured and reinforced.

Yet Lorenzo Albacete never feared engaging with those who did not believe. He was respectful of their questioning and sought to enter into a real dialogue with them, just as Pope Francis is always urging us to do.

The problem of evil and the suffering of the innocent are often huge obstacles to embracing the faith. Lorenzo found the response to these questions in the book of the cross.

Science can answer many questions about the world around us, but it cannot tell us the value of things, our own identity, our purpose and mission. These things can be discovered only by faith, a faith nurtured by prayer. In today's world, pain is seen as the new sin that needs to be eliminated. Ironically enough, many of our contemporaries are convinced that when life is difficult or inconvenient it should be eliminated. The governments in our Western democracies are constantly moving the goalposts of protection for human life. Individuals strive to avoid pain and stress by turning to alcohol, drugs, and reckless sexual behaviors.

So great is the horror of bodily pain that annually billions of dollars in our country are spent by those who can afford it to avoid pain or to lessen it. It is not just our bodies that suffer; there is pain in the human soul to be rejected by those we love. To be misunderstood and worse still to be misrepresented is painful. If we are passed over when others are chosen, or ignored when others are recognized or praised, or forgotten when others are remembered, it can be painful. To make mistakes and as a consequence to be embarrassed or ashamed, or to do what is wrong and then have to live with the memory of our sins, is always painful.

It is comforting to see in the Gospels that an important part of Jesus's ministry is alleviating people's pain, the pain in their bodies and in their souls. In a fascinating study of how Jesus managed his time, it was revealed that Jesus spent most of his time caring for the sick and performing works of mercy. It is obvious that he does not cure everyone or eliminate all disease or suffering. In many ways, he comes to share our suffering, our hunger and fatigue, our loneliness, and our pain in the bodily pain of his passion and crucifixion, but also in the psychological pain of the agony in the garden: the pain of being betrayed, the pain of being abandoned.

Jesus comes among us as the suffering servant, and by his stripes, we are healed. The very symbol of our Christian faith is the cross which is an instrument of torture and death. For those who see Christianity from outside, the cross is a puzzling symbol. We should ask ourselves how we would react if we saw someone hanging a replica of a guillotine or an electric chair on the wall of their home and that gruesome symbol was supposed to represent their religion. Yet that is precisely what we do, because Jesus has transformed the cross into a symbol of victory and hope.

Indeed St. Francis said the cross was the book where he was able to read the greatest love story in history. On the cross, Jesus shows us by his passion and death how profitable prayerful suffering can be. The most important single lesson humankind has to learn is the meaning of suffering and its value. It took God to teach us. And He has to resort to the extreme expedient of becoming man and suffering Himself to prove to us that suffering is not meaningless and that it is one of the most valuable experiences in human life.

The cross is a two-edged sword. Without prayer, the cross becomes death and destruction. It can cause us to turn in on ourselves, to be blind to the sufferings of others, to be filled with self-pity, to be enraged, to be jealous of those who are not suffering, to be bitter, and to despair. When the cross is borne with love, it becomes life-giving, increasing our capacity for love and empathy; it allows us to be united with Christ in love and to witness to his power in our lives.

Bonhoeffer spoke about cheap grace and costly grace. We live in a world where many are pandering to the merchants of cheap grace. The grace of discipleship is a costly grace and comes when we embrace the cross. When St. Peter fled from Gethsemane, he tried to follow Jesus at a safe distance, when suddenly he was identified by his accent. The frightened Peter denies even knowing Jesus, and not to a soldier with a long spear, but to a waitress with an attitude. Eventually, Peter discovers that the only way to follow Jesus is not at a safe distance but up close.

In a world chasing after cheap grace and instant mysticism with all sorts of fads and gimmicks presented as means of becoming "one with the absolute," it is helpful to reflect on the words of Ignatius of Loyola:

> If God gives you an abundant harvest of trials, it is a sign of great holiness which he desires you to attain. Do you want to become a great saint? Ask God to send you many sufferings. The flame of divine love never rises higher than when fed with the wood of the Cross, which the infinite charity of the Savior used to finish his sacrifice. All the pleasures of the world are nothing compared to the sweetness found in the gall and vinegar offered to Jesus Christ, that is, hard and painful things endured for Jesus Christ and with Jesus Christ.

Lorenzo Albacete's profound reflections are teaching us how to say yes to the life-giving cross, to find meaning in the mystery, and to be able to read in the cross the greatest love story ever told.

— Cardinal Seán O'Malley

I

A Mystery to Be Lived

I WOULD NEVER ATTEMPT to offer an answer to the problem that suffering poses to believers. Suffering is not a problem to be solved but a mystery to be lived. As a Catholic Christian, I see the problem of suffering as inseparable from the cross of Jesus. But this is not the perspective I have adopted here, because I do not wish to begin by speaking only to other Christians. I want to start by reflecting on experiences we all have because we are human beings, whatever our beliefs.

I remember what François Mauriac, the French Catholic writer, wrote in his introduction to Elie Wiesel's *The Night Trilogy*. As a young journalist for a Tel Aviv newspaper, Wiesel had interviewed Mauriac. Soon they were engaged in a personal conversation about the Holocaust. Mauriac told Wiesel that his wife said she'd witnessed Jewish children at the Austerlitz train station being torn away from their mothers, and even though she didn't know what awaited them in the camps, she was horrified. Mauriac writes:

I believe that on that day I touched for the first time upon the mystery of iniquity whose revelation was to mark the end of an era and the beginning of another. The dream which Western man conceived in the eighteenth century, whose dawn he thought he saw in 1789 [the beginning of the French Revolution], and which, until August 2, 1914, had grown stronger with the progress of enlightenment and the discoveries of science—this dream vanished finally for me before those trainloads of little children. And yet I was still thousands of miles away from thinking that they were to be fuel for the gas chamber and the crematory.

Mauriac cannot help but think of the religious implications of this horror. In his introduction, he writes about Wiesel's own experience:

The child who tells us his story here was one of God's elect. From the time when his conscience first awoke, he had lived only for God and had been reared only on the Talmud, aspiring to initiation into the cabbala, dedicated to the Eternal. Have we ever thought about the consequences of a horror that, though less apparent, less striking than the other outrages, is yet the worst of all to those of us who have faith: the death of God in the soul of a child who suddenly discovers absolute evil?

Wiesel's own words about his experience are overwhelming: "Never shall I forget those flames which consumed my Faith forever.... Never shall I forget those moments which murdered my God and my soul and turned my dreams into dust. Never shall I forget these things, even if I am condemned to live as long as God

Himself. Never." These words are not fiction or hyperbole. They are real life.

Recalling his presence as a child at the feast of Rosh Hashanah, Wiesel writes: "That day, I had ceased to plead, I was no longer capable of lamentation. On the contrary, I felt very strong. I was the accuser, and God the accused. My eyes were open and I was alone—terribly alone in a world without God and without man. Without love or mercy. I had ceased to be anything but ashes, yet I felt myself to be stronger than the Almighty, to whom my life had been tied for so long."

Every fiber of my own heart vibrates with this anguished protest. I too would join Wiesel, Mauriac, and all who have experienced such horrors in cursing this face of the Infinite. And yet, there is something else in my heart that will also not go away—the certainty that this anger cannot be, and cannot be allowed to be, the last word about human life.

The last word must be the hope of the same heart that causes me still to protest, to rail against the infinite Mystery that permits such horrors to happen.

Accusation...and Acknowledgment

In the program "The Millennial Pope," Germaine Greer speaks movingly about suffering and God, and I was asked to respond to her cry. Although a self-proclaimed atheist, Greer, with tears in her eyes, movingly expressed her deep appreciation for religious music as a human cry towards a presence that was "just not there." Then, in the face of the sufferings of children in Africa, she added: "If God exists, I hate him."

What could I possibly say in response? Not only would a prepackaged religious reply have been insulting, but I also found an echo of her words within me. I knew her words came from her heart. I thought they were, in the truest sense of the word, authentic—honestly reflecting the author who had uttered them. I remembered that the existentialist writer and philosopher Jean-Paul Sartre had seen such personal authenticity as a kind of sanctity. Germaine Greer is that kind of saint. I hope she doesn't mind the appellation. I use it to show my respect for those who, in the face of human suffering, cannot believe in God.

As a striving towards transcendence, creative suffering—as we've seen expressed in Germaine Greer's anguished words—opens us to others who are also suffering, thus creating a solidarity among those who suffer. To suffer together means to walk together towards transcendence. This solidarity is the proper human response to suffering. This doesn't mean that we "share the pain" of those who suffer. While this phrase is used quite often, I don't think this is possible. Nothing is more intimately personal than the pain of suffering. It is, after all, a wound in our personal identity, and personal identity cannot be shared. Each person is unique and unrepeatable. What we share is the questioning—and thus we suffer with the one who suffers. We *co-suffer* with that person.

Since suffering reflects the transcendence of the human person, since it points to a Mystery that is the author of the drama of human life, then we cannot really use suffering to deny the existence of God. Instead, it is because there is a God that suffering exists as human beings experience it. The suffering of human beings is a sign of God.

What this God is like is another question.

I am reminded of C.S. Lewis's autobiographical *A Grief Observed*. He wrote about his suffering as a result of his wife's death (and her suffering in the struggle against it, especially when her hopes, raised by what appeared to be miraculous interventions, were dashed by a worsening of her illness). This suffering did not make him doubt God's existence; rather, it made him doubt God's goodness. If the meaning of suffering cannot be grasped, this response in the face of unbearable suffering is understandable. But both Lewis's and Greer's comments are at once both accusation and acknowledgment of transcendence.

Co-suffering and the Unutterable Question

It is no surprise that, according to some scripture scholars, the Gospel of John presents Jesus's suffering as a trial in which God is the accused. Satan is the accuser, and we are the jury. To co-suffer is to be willing to serve on the jury in the trial of God and to risk our own faith by identifying with those who suffer in their questioning of God. Even if the one who suffers can no longer articulate or express the experience of suffering, we must put that unutterable question into words for those who suffer. We must establish that solidarity, risk our own faith and identity, make a human connection with the sufferer, and cry out to God together.

Authentic suffering, then, is a dialogue, not only with God but also among humans. To co-suffer is to share the question *why*, to be a companion, and to walk together towards transcendence.

The one who does not co-suffer and is not prepared to do so cannot speak about suffering. Such a person does not know the truth and does not speak the truth. That person is a "liar" or a "deceiver," to use the words of Walker Percy. The only adequate response when confronted with another person's suffering is co-suffering. It is the only way to respect the suffering of another. Co-suffering affirms the wounded personal identity of the sufferer through our willingness to expose our identity to the questioning provoked by the sufferer's pain. This willingness to share suffering is an act of love.

Co-suffering is the way we love the one who suffers.

In our relationship with the one who suffers, we as co-sufferers can impose nothing on the other person. We can only help the other to ask the question "why" by asking it together — that is, by praying together. Praying together with the one who suffers is the just response to suffering.

The cruelest response to suffering is the attempt to explain it away, to tell the one who suffers: "This is why this is happening. I'm sorry that you can't see the answer, but it's clear to me." When the apostles saw a man born blind, for example, they asked Jesus whether it was due to his sins or his parents' sins. Jesus rejected this explanation: he does not suffer because of his sins or his parents' sins, but to manifest God's glory.

To look for an answer in the past is to reduce suffering to a functional problem. The functional mentality explains everything in terms of past causes. This does not do justice to the one who suffers. I call this the "secularization" of suffering, the elimination of its link with transcendence. Job's friends sought to explain the origins of Job's suffering by looking to his past, but Job bitterly protested and repeatedly rejected those explanations as, at the end of the book, God also did. Philosopher Martin Heidegger said that pious persons are not the ones who recognize themselves as guilty before God when they suffer but the ones who struggle against God.

Something Always Greater Than Us

What emerges from the struggle with God? Mystery's answer to suffering is always grace—a free grace that comes to us without conditions, without rationalizations, without explanations. Suffering can be relieved by the co-sufferer only when the co-sufferer can bring the suffering person into contact with grace and into the experience of being loved. The answer to suffering will always be an experience of grace and love.

For Job's so-called friends, Job's suffering was an occasion to construct their theology rather than an opportunity to express their love. They would not walk with him, co-suffer with him, pray with him for grace. Instead, they fit Job's suffering into a theological system that explained everything away. True friends would have acknowledged the horror he was going through, stood by him in his pain, and refrained from offering an answer to or a reason for his suffering. Since suffering is experienced as a destruction that renders life meaningless, simplistic explanations trivialize the suffering. It's like saying those who suffer lose their right to full life because of something they did and now they have to pay the price.

Job understood that he could not accept an explanation for his suffering; to do so would have devalued his own life and experience.

With grace, we suddenly experience the goodness of our (and others') existence, which has infinite value for its own sake. At the end of the Book of Job, God asks Job to consider his origins, to realize that he was created without any claim to existence, that he is not his own maker. His existence is sheer grace. Job discovers himself when he is asked by God to consider the mystery of his human identity. By asking questions of Job, God joins, so to speak, Job's questioning. In a way, God co-suffers with Job.

Suffering is an expression of human personhood, human transcendence. God's response to our suffering—a suffering with us—respects our identity as individuals. Likewise, the most intimate encounter between human beings is through shared suffering. The communion of life born through shared suffering is the strongest interpersonal communion in the world, breaking down all barriers among human beings, and bringing us together through a bond with transcendence, with "something always greater than us."

Born from the Flesh

Emmanuel Mounier, the founder of the French "personalist" philosophical movement, wrote that the most important aspect of human life is a "divine restlessness" in us, a divine "lack of peace" within our hearts. It is a permanent search for the meaning of life, an interest imprinted on "un-extinguished souls," on those who are not paralyzed by temporary satisfactions or ideological answers to all human questions. Indeed what makes our lives truly human is the ceaseless questioning before Mystery, before "something greater," whether we are three or ninety-three years old. This questioning allows us to see even everyday sights with the same amazement and wonder we felt the first time we saw them and to keep our hearts awake to the world around us.

This questioning also makes life worth living in the midst of even the greatest sufferings. Mounier saw those united by this approach to life as constituting a unique community, a people committed to action, to new initiatives that break ground at the deepest level of human experience and open new possibilities for humankind. The inhabitants of the world of suffering are the ones who truly transform the world. They are the true revolutionaries on behalf of human dignity. He writes of those he had met through such experience:

> I have always thought that we would endure, by virtue of the organic character of our beginnings: It is from the earth, from its solidarity, that a birth full of joy takes place ... and a patient feeling of a work that grows, of the stages that follow, awaited almost calmly, with assuredness (in the midst of the discomfort of days of anguish). It is necessary to suffer so that the truth not be crystallized in doctrine, but be born from the flesh.

For Mounier, these words were not mere abstractions—he lived them. For years he and his wife desired a child, but when their daughter finally arrived, she suffered from a terrible brain disease, which left her disfigured. The care of the child affected every moment of their lives, day after day. "I feel a great tiredness," he wrote, "and at the same time a great calm mixed together. I think that the real, the positive, are given in the calm, by the love of our child being sweetly transformed into an offering, in a tenderness that surpasses her, originates in her, and returns to her, transforming us with her."

In his profound suffering, he turns to the Mystery from which suffering originates and makes a pilgrimage to a place of miracles, begging for a miracle, but not the miracle of having the illness cured. He asks to come home again with the sick child and "know the joy of having believed in the gratuity of the grace of God [and not in its automatic therapeutical effects], the joy of knowing that a miracle is never refused to one who accepts in advance whatever form it will have when given, even if it were invisible, even if it had a crucified form, even if it were a matter of a misfortune. Instead, it is not a matter of a misfortune. We have been visited by Someone very great."

We Have Been Visited by Someone Very Great

"We have been visited by Someone very great"—this is the deepest experience of which human persons are capable before the mystery of suffering. The "misfortune" becomes a claim to go beyond pure resignation to an active commitment—to "remain with you," as he says to his daughter. Co-suffering makes us stand before those who suffer with profound awe and respect. In these experiences, "Someone very great" visits us.

And still, as we consider earlier reflections, we must ask: What about Germaine Greer? What about Elie Wiesel? As we saw earlier, Greer and Wiesel also experienced something "very great" indeed, and it was an absolute horror.

Adam Phillips tells the story of John Cage, who attended a concert of works composed by a friend. The friend had also written the program notes, in which he said that he hoped his music would help diminish the suffering in the world. After the concert, Cage told his friend that he loved the music but hated the program notes. He didn't think there was "too much" suffering in the world. As far as he was concerned, there was the "right amount." Indeed, ideas such as "too much" or "too little" show that someone measures according to a standard. But what if there is no standard? What if the world is what it is because that's the way it all works out when all the forces of nature interact with each other at this moment in its evolution? Then concepts like "too little" merely indicate taste or preference, those manifestations of "nature" that we do or don't like.

There is no way of responding to Cage's position other than to recognize that the deepest demands of the human heart somehow go beyond "nature" as defined by science, since in such a view of nature, the amount of suffering in the world is, precisely as Cage notes, always just what it has to be. Inasmuch as suffering admits of no "explanations," unless we can figure out something more to say, Cage has a point indeed.

And yet, we must also acknowledge Mounier's experience—both the tremendous suffering that he, his wife, and his daughter experienced, as well as the tremendous grace. Somehow to accept without question the suffering of the Mounier family seems heartless, and to deny the grace they experienced is spiritless. We face the realization that, if we are truly alive, we will always be divinely restless—filled with both the mystery of questions as well as the mystery of grace that we cannot comprehend without a spirit of faith.

No theory or explanation about the origin of suffering—be it cosmic, evolutionary, other-worldly, historical, or the result of human action—can satisfy the human heart, where suffering is experienced as offensive to existence itself. In that sense, the origin of suffering is something irrational, where rational indicates the human capacity to make sense of it. It is not something merely unknown, but unknowable, a break in the fabric of understanding itself. No cause can explain it adequately.

I suppose that the most popular explanation of suffering is that it is the result of individual or collective guilt, a punishment for doing something that should not have been done ("sin"). Given the universality and longevity of this view, something about it must correspond within human experience. After all, the experience of guilt and the suffering it provokes is the driving force behind most religions. That is why "innocent suffering" is so scandalous and such a threat to religion.

The Rebellion of Ivan Karamazov

But if we admit that all explanations concerning the origins of suffering are unacceptable, then isn't all suffering really innocent suffering? Isn't that the point, in Dostoyevsky's The Brothers Karamazov, of Ivan Karamazov's argument? We will do well to recall his words. Rejecting the consolation that, at the end of history, we will somehow restore the harmony wounded by a child's suffering, he cries out: "Can they be redeemed by being avenged? But what do I care if they are avenged, what do I care if the tormentors are in hell, what can hell set right here? I want to forgive, and I want to embrace. I don't want more suffering. And if the suffering of children goes to make up the sum of suffering needed to buy truth, then I assert beforehand that the whole truth is not worth such a price.... I don't want harmony, for love of mankind I don't want it. I want to remain with unrequited suffering.... They have put too high a price on harmony; we can't afford to pay so much for admission."

Who of us has never felt some sympathy for this stunning protest, echoing it in the deepest region of our heart? And the question stands: Why this heart-rending protest? Who put it there? The rebellion of Ivan Karamazov is at least as mysterious as the suffering he decries. Human nature is not the origin of evil and suffering. Evil is something totally alien to the way we are made, to our identity as persons. The myth of original man and woman in paradise reveals far more of how we are made than the evil and suffering that has been inseparable from history as we know it. The fact that the "man and woman of prehistory" lacked knowledge of good and evil does not make them less human than us — it makes them more human. It is because evil is so alien to how we are made that suffering and death are so repulsive. We cannot imagine history without the struggle that brings about suffering, but deep within our hearts we hear a distant echo of what could have been, of how human life was really meant to be.

Suffering, we said, puts us in the presence of, in Mounier's words, "Someone very great." But if this is so, if this "Someone very great" is not to be the origin of the horrors experienced, then this Someone must be one who can descend into the hell we have encountered. This Someone must be able and willing to enter into a relationship with us that will prevent us from sinking into the absolute loneliness that is hell. This Someone must be capable of love even in hell, for hell is not to love anymore.

The redemption of suffering and the mystery of love are inseparable. The response to suffering is not to stop caring—that, in fact, is hell—but to experience a caring that sustains us in our humanity as it was meant to be. This is the redemption that the heart seeks.

A Child and His Mother

The following example should help us understand the argument. A little boy falls down while playing and scratches his knees and arms. For a brief moment, he stays down on the pavement as if considering his condition. Then he looks around and sees his mother at a distance. He gets up and, crying loudly—as if in the most agonizing despair—he runs into his mother's arms. She kisses and consoles him with soothing remarks. The child's cry seems first to intensify, as if coming from deep inside his soul, but then it winds down rapidly. It is not surprising that, within a couple of minutes, he is even smiling. The wounds remain untreated—the pain has not disappeared—but something has happened such that the child is no longer suffering. Why?

Human suffering has two dimensions: subjective and objective. In our example above, the objective suffering of the child clearly relates to the pain of his scratches. This is the physical source of suffering. There is, though, another aspect to this suffering. Let us call it the psychological one. In our example, it would be the pain of not being able to continue playing—or the embarrassment, maybe, of being seen falling down.

Yet this is still not all. There is something else experienced for the first time, perhaps during those moments of surprise before the child cries. Yes, it could be that the child, frightened by his fall, has not fully realized what has happened. But I don't think this is all. In whatever way we can imagine it in a small child, his surprise also contains a perception of injustice, of unfairness. This should not happen. Why do these things happen?

Perhaps this wondering, this protest, intensified when he noticed his mother because she reminds him of everything that is good and beautiful in life as he knows it. That, precisely, is why he begins to cry then. Some might think it is only to call attention to himself. I suggest that this is not all. His cry is also a cry of protest, and, for the moment, his mother's attention (when he sees her and when she begins to comfort him) intensifies this protest. However, this is what his mother's love has conquered. For, in the end, suffering is transformed by love.

The little child in our example is right: he should not have fallen down. Little children playing should not fall down and get hurt. Awareness of this little, perhaps insignificant, evil is but a hint of what can really happen in this world: the suffering of children dying of famine or in a natural disaster. Moral suffering, the experience of this evil, cannot be dealt with by physical and psychological therapies. Moral suffering is ultimately perceived as an absurdity: the why of evil can neither be answered within the physical nor even psychological orders because evil has its roots in something beyond.

That is why human suffering cannot be totally relieved by medicine and psychotherapy. It can appear to be so if the immediate occasion for suffering can be removed or if its deepest dimension is suppressed. But this is not real healing. Real healing takes place when the spiritual dimension of suffering is dealt with. This is why healthcare appropriate for human beings must seek the *relief of suffering* which may occur *even if it is not possible to relieve physical or psychological pain directly*. How is this done?

We can begin to understand this by returning to our example of the little child. Nothing was done by his mother to heal his physical pain. Whatever psychological suffering the child is enduring has not been treated directly. His mother need not say anything intelligible to him; in fact, if she tried to explain to him that he should have been more careful or how it is that the ground is slippery for some reason or another, the child probably would cry even more.

What the mother does touches the depths of his suffering. She touches and soothes the wound in his soul. She does this by affirming the relation of love between the two of them. Love enables her to share her son's burdens and thus to lighten them, indeed, to lift them altogether. This interior healing touch made possible by her love relieves even her son's psychological and physical suffering.

The Freedom to Love

Love, though, is impossible without freedom; but freedom allows the possibility of acting against love. The freedom to love is what allows the human being to escape the limitations of what science calls nature and to experience justice and injustice.

There is an experience of freedom that is especially revealing. I feel free when my needs are fulfilled in all their dimensions and manifestations. Freedom, therefore, is the capacity for perfection, the capacity for being made perfect.

But we know very well that nothing ever satisfies us in such a way that we'll never desire more of it or something else. Our hearts desire infinite happiness, infinite satisfaction. Freedom is the capacity for infinity. I am free each time I walk along the path that moves me to infinity, to the stars. If I choose to act in a particular way that separates me from my infinite destiny, I lose something of my freedom and move closer to that abyss of not being free, that is, of "not being able to love anymore." I can be rescued only when the attraction of infinity wins over whatever is attracting me away from it. This is the redemption of my freedom.

The redemption of suffering, inseparable from the drama of freedom, must also take the form of the attractive, loving presence of that "Someone very great" who leads me to the infinity of which I've lost sight. This Someone is willing to co-suffer with me and sustain me as capable of infinity — that is, as free. Whatever the Mystery of my origin and destiny is like, it must somehow possess and be defined by this capacity to sustain my freedom to love through co-suffering. If I call this Mystery "God," then somehow the identity of God must be expressed as the Infinite Love revealed through co-suffering with humankind.

A Transforming Event

Suffering can be redeemed only by grace, by a love that is recognized as unconditional, boundless, infinite. Paradoxically, the drama of innocent suffering that can move us to deny God and hate the very possibility of God's existence can also lead us to discover God. To co-suffer, though, means to risk our identity, and the God who redeems us from suffering must also be willing and able to take that risk, of appearing to us as "nondivine" or different from the absolute power that we associate with divinity. As the Jewish philosopher Emmanuel Levinas said, if there is to be an "incarnation of Transcendence," it can only take the form of absolute humility.

Human beings can humbly co-suffer with those whom they love, but, in the end, this co-suffering can only be limited. Our identity, so to speak, is not strong enough to fully sustain the identity of the one who suffers. In the end, human love by itself is always confronted with death. You cannot love someone so much that you can prevent that person from dying. But what if the co-sufferer is the author of our identity? Then this co-suffering would be stronger than death.

Redemption by "divine" co-suffering, therefore, is not a matter of justice rectifying the injustice of suffering, as Ivan Karamazov imagined. Such categories make no sense if love is the ultimate word about the drama of human existence. But if human existence is not about love, then it is not about freedom either. In that case, Cage's observation that there's just the right amount of suffering in the world would be the right answer to the horror experienced by Ivan Karamazov, Germaine Greer, Elie Wiesel, and the many, many others who in the past century alone have come across the mystery of iniquity that is hell.

The redemption of suffering, as our experience indicates, cannot be found as an "ultimate answer" to a problem: it can only be an event that transforms the drama of suffering into a drama of love and shows love to be more powerful than its denial. The possibility of this event sustains a realistic hope and an unfailing determination to protect and defend human freedom and the dignity of human life.

Redemption does not eliminate suffering. Indeed, just as suffering creates a "world" of suffering, so does the redemption of suffering create a community of those who love and offer a home to those who suffer. Its presence in the world of suffering represents an invitation to free human beings to embrace a new vocation, a new mission: to join the community of "redemptive suffering," to help complete what may be lacking in its inner resources to offer a home to those who suffer, sparing them from the loneliness that is hell.

We began with François Mauriac's comments concerning Elie Wiesel, and it is appropriate to return to Mauriac as we close our discussion of suffering. I understand fully Mauriac's observations about his meeting with Wiesel. Mauriac writes:

What did I say to him? Did I speak of that other Israeli, his brother who may have resembled him—the Crucified, whose Cross has conquered the world? Did I affirm that the stumbling block to his faith was the cornerstone of mine, and that the conformity between the Cross and the suffering of men was in my eyes the key to that impenetrable mystery whereon the faith of his childhood had perished?...We do not know the worth of one single drop of blood, one single tear. All is grace. If the Eternal is the Eternal, the last word for each one of us belongs to Him. This is what I should have told this Jewish child. But I could only embrace him, weeping.

2

You Cannot Love
What Shocks You

WHAT I WOULD LIKE TO DO now is to reflect on the reality of suffering as the light of faith allows us to see it. We must see it in a certain way if we are to respond to it from the standpoint of faith. One area where this has a particular application lies in the realm of Catholic healthcare, which depends on an understanding of the problems we face from the light of faith—this understanding will give to the ministry of healthcare the uniqueness that the world desperately needs, has always needed, but even more so now. In addition, I would like to examine the contemporary culture in which we live, because the insights about suffering that come from faith will help us respond to what is otherwise a deeply mistaken approach to dealing with human suffering.

"Tenderness leads to the gas chamber." This is a quote from a novel by Walker Percy called *The Thanatos Syndrome*, published in 1987. Anyone involved in healthcare ought to read this book in order to understand the context in which you discharge your work and follow your ministry today. The point to be made is that, in the light of the immense suffering of the world, we have a clash between two distinct approaches: "tenderness" versus the redemption of suffering.

Percy's words are an echo of an insight by the great Southern novelist Flannery O'Connor in the "Introduction to *A Memoir of Mary Anne*" from her essay collection *Mystery and Manners*. Flannery O'Connor was asked by the Sister Superior of Our Lady of Perpetual Help Free Cancer Home in Atlanta to write the story of a young girl who had been admitted with incurable cancer at age three and died of her disease when she was twelve. She was born with a tumor on the side of her face that caused her to lose one eye. Apparently, Mary Ann had an enormous impact on the life of the home, and the sisters wanted to capture their experience of those nine years, so they asked Flannery O'Connor to write about her. O'Connor's response was characteristically unsentimental: "Stories of pious children tend to be false." She suggested that the sisters write it themselves and offered to edit it and write an introduction.

Wisdom from Hawthorne and his Daughter

The congregation in charge of the home where Mary Ann lived was called Servants for the Relief of Incurable Cancer, founded by Mother Mary Alphonsa, the daughter of Nathaniel Hawthorne, the renowned author of *The Scarlet Letter*. When Flannery O'Connor learned this, she immediately re-read one of Hawthorne's short stories called "The Birthmark." In that story, there is a man named Aylmer who has a wife, Georgiana, who has what he thinks is a rather ugly-looking birthmark on her face. He has never told her he finds her birthmark repellent.

> One day, very soon after their marriage, Aylmer sat gazing at his wife with a trouble in his countenance that grew stronger until he spoke.
>
> "Georgiana," said he, "has it never occurred to you that the mark upon your cheek might be removed?"
>
> "No, indeed," said she, smiling; but perceiving the seriousness of his manner, she blushed deeply. "To tell you the truth it has been so often called a charm that I was simple enough to imagine it might be so."
>
> "Ah, upon another face perhaps it might," replied her husband; "but never on yours. No, dearest Georgiana, you came so nearly perfect from the hand of Nature that this slightest possible defect, which we hesitate whether to term a defect or a beauty, shocks me, as being the visible mark of earthly imperfection."
>
> "Shocks you, my husband!" cried Georgiana, deeply hurt; at first reddening with momentary anger, but then bursting into tears. "Then why did you take me from my mother's side? You cannot love what shocks you!"

This quote contains the key point Flannery O'Connor wants to make, namely: "You cannot love what shocks you." This woman lost faith in her husband's love for her, because it turns out that he was shocked by a physical defect. He says, "you came so nearly perfect from the hand of Nature," that he felt a desperate need to remove this imperfection. It appears that she was so beautiful otherwise that this mark was disturbing to him, and he wanted to remove it.

O'Connor remarks how Hawthorne himself was apparently a man who struggled with the same problem as Aylmer. She refers to still another story called "Our Old Home" in which Hawthorne describes the efforts of "a fastidious gentleman" who was followed by a wretched child so awful-looking that he could not decide what sex it was. When the poor child reached out its arms to the man to be held, he reluctantly picked it up and held it. Hawthorne comments:

> It could be no easy thing for him to do, he being a person burdened with more than an Englishman's customary reserve, shy of actual contact with human beings, afflicted with a peculiar distaste for whatever was ugly, and, furthermore, accustomed to that habit of observation from an insulated stand-point which is said (but, I hope, erroneously) to have the tendency of putting ice into the blood. So I watched the struggle in his mind with a good deal of interest, and am seriously of the opinion that he did an heroic act, and effected more than he dreamed of towards his final salvation, when he took up the loathsome child and caressed it as tenderly as if he had been its father.

The Good Is Always under Construction

In some of the notebooks published after Hawthorne's death, it turns out that this incident was biographical, that this had occurred to Hawthorne himself, and that he actually had had to struggle with the repulsion at reaching out to this thing that was so ugly and so deformed. However, Hawthorne did pick up the child. In so doing, he overcame his shock and repulsion. Unlike Aylmer in "The Birthmark," whose only solution to what he regarded as a deformity was surgery, the fastidious gentleman in "Our Old Home" recognized that he had a spiritual problem, that there was something within him that was not right, even if he didn't fully understand it. Despite this limitation, he knew he had to accept the child as he was.

O'Connor says that Rose, Hawthorne's daughter, deliberately modeled the community of sisters she founded on her father's short story, to minister to the incurable. According to O'Connor, the sisters "were shocked at nothing and ... loved life so much that they spent their own lives making comfortable those who had been pronounced incurable of cancer."

I think the refusal to be shocked or repulsed in the face of suffering is the calling of every Christian. We have to reach out to those who suffer with a profound acceptance of their agony instead of seeking to remove or destroy their experience. We cannot be blind to suffering; we cannot isolate those who suffer, nor can we use medical science to destroy the sufferer when our attempt to cure the disease has failed.

Many people came to that house and visited with Mary Anne, O'Connor says, and they were perhaps told when they left to think of how thankful they should be that God had made their faces straight. Then she comments, "It is doubtful if any of them were as fortunate as Mary Anne." O'Connor accounts for why some people are shocked by disfigurement and others are not, concluding that it is because those who are not shocked are somehow able to recognize the presence of goodness or even a kind of beauty. The face of good, says O'Connor, is grotesque in human beings. Good in us, she says, is always something under construction, and when confronted with the shocking, the task should be to use it to construct good rather than to eliminate it. In this way, we make something good in the midst of imperfection.

Mary Anne died, and Flannery O'Connor comments as follows:

> Bishop Hyland preached Mary Anne's funeral sermon. He said that the world would ask why Mary Anne should die.... The Bishop was speaking to her family and friends. He could not have been thinking of that world much farther removed yet everywhere, which would not ask why Mary Anne should die but why she should be born in the first place.
>
> One of the tendencies of our age is to use the suffering of children to discredit the goodness of God. And once you have discredited His goodness, you are done with him. The Aylmers, whom Hawthorne saw as a menace have multiplied. Busy cutting down human imperfection, they are making headway also on the raw material of good. Ivan Karamazov cannot believe, as long as one child is in torment. Camus's hero cannot accept the divinity of Christ because of the massacre of the innocents. In this popular pity, we mark our gain in sensibility and our loss in vision. If other ages felt less, they saw more, even though they saw with the blind, prophetical, unsentimental eye of acceptance, which is to say, of faith. In this absence of this faith now, we govern by tenderness. It is a tenderness

which, long since cut off from the person of Christ, is wrapped in theory. When tenderness is detached from the source of tenderness, its logical outcome is terror. It ends in forced labor camps and in the fumes of the gas chamber.

Two Types of Sorrow

When we feel sorry for the afflicted because they diverge from our notion of perfection, our sorrow is destructive. O'Connor calls it "popular pity." She is not saying that we should not feel sorrow for someone's suffering. But she is asking us to examine what kind of sorrow we feel and what our notion of a solution is. She is saying that this "popular pity" has led to a loss in vision, the inability to see any good in suffering. Other ages, she says, were more used to the grotesque, and this somehow led them to see more because they saw with the eyes of faith. She calls this faith the "blind, prophetical, unsentimental eye of acceptance." Instead of faith, we have sentimentality, tenderness, and theory. If we have lost the ability to attach suffering to the person of the suffering Christ, then suffering becomes merely a problem to be fixed, a disfigurement to be removed. It is this impulse that leads to the gas chambers.

A phrase most often used by the purveyors of tenderness is "quality of life." This is a very dangerous concept. When we no longer see the goodness of the life of people who are totally helpless, totally dependent, and who may even be suffering, we feel that the only solution to their suffering is to put them to death. However understandable it is to want someone's suffering to end, our pity becomes evil when it has become detached from the source of tenderness, which is the person of Christ.

The insight that the medical establishment—the healthcare establishment as we know it today—is governed by false tenderness and is subsequently destroying lives is the subject of the futuristic novel *The Thanatos Syndrome* by Walker Percy. The particular incident around which the book is based is an experiment being done through a secret arrangement between members of a medical community and some people in the federal government in order to eliminate crime. The scientists secretly put chemicals in the town's water supply that supposedly will reduce violence, greed, and other ills. And initially it works: human imperfection is indeed being eliminated, turning the town into an idyllic community. The problem is that many other things are also disappearing—the capacity for commitment, for shock, for anger. The protagonist Tom More, a psychiatrist and agnostic who has been in jail for selling prescription drugs, notices that something is going wrong, and he sets out to find out what.

Tom More is aided by a crazy old priest named Fr. Smith who lives on top of a tower watching for fires (a sly allusion to St. Simeon Stylites). His bishop has assigned him to a parish, but he never shows up. Fr. Smith serves as the spokesperson for Percy's critique of contemporary society. Percy purposely chooses a person who everyone considers insane, because he wants to show how the Church understands and responds to human imperfection and suffering and that this response is increasingly outside the mainstream "tender" response of contemporary healthcare.

"Tenderness" Leads to the Gas Chamber

Fr. Smith, in his explanation of what's disturbing him, echoes one of Percy's main critiques of today's culture. Percy says in one of his essays, "Words have been deprived of their meaning. We have had a change of language, or rather a change of meaning of the same words." What is this "devaluation of language"? It's a bit like the devaluation of currency. The bill looks the same, but it's not worth as much. The words are the same, but they don't mean the same. The meaning which words used to possess in the West—largely influenced by biblical faith—has been taken away, and we have lost the value of recognizing certain signs. Percy calls this an "evacuation of signs." Language—which is a system of signs—no longer mediates reality as it once did. In order to make language fit what O'Connor identified as a loss of vision—or faith—there is an attempt to redesign contemporary culture, to remake reality. And when this cannot be done, when some things like suffering and sin refuse to go away, then the tendency is to attempt to destroy the cause.

Along these lines, Percy brings up the example of the Jews. Somehow, the Jews refuse to go away, and they remain as a thorn in the side of many. The priest says that the Jews have been persecuted because of the unique relationship of that people with God. And so every effort is made to secularize, to devalue that unique relationship. But when that effort fails, then the Holocaust follows.

This is what Fr. Smith tells Tom More. He gives his own example of a doctor he knew in Germany who was driven to tears by the suffering of children. The priest knew him before World War II, and, at the end of the war, he found that he was one of the head doctors in a concentration camp that used Jewish children for medical experiments in order to find out ways of helping other, presumably Aryan, children. The priest says,

> If you are a lover of Mankind in the abstract like Walt Whitman, who wished the best for Mankind, you will probably do no harm and might even write good poetry and give pleasure....
>
> If you are a theorist of Mankind like Rousseau or Skinner, who believes he understands man's brain and in the solitariness of his study or laboratory writes books on the subject, you are also probably harmless and might even contribute to human knowledge....
>
> But if you put the two together, a lover of Mankind and a theorist of Mankind, what you've got now is Robespierre or Stalin or Hitler and the Terror, and millions dead for the good of Mankind.

Note how this is the same point Flannery O'Connor makes when she says, "When tenderness is detached from the source of tenderness [Christ], its logical outcome is terror." Both Percy and O'Connor believe this is clearly a satanic work. When Percy talks about words being deprived of their meaning, the priest talks about the Great Depriver who is warring against humanity.

At the end of The Thanatos Syndrome, when all the mysteries are solved and somehow this priest is able to put together a healthcare facility for those patients nobody wants, a Mass is held. All kinds of important people are there—journalists, medical doctors, politicians, and so forth—and the priest kind of staggers in (perhaps he has had a little drink beforehand) to say Mass. The following is part of his homily:

> Listen to me dear physicians, dear brothers, dear Qualitarians, abortionists, euthanasists. Do you know why you are going to listen to me? Because every last one of you is a better person than I and you know it. Yet, you like me. Every last one of you knows me and what I am, a failed priest, an old drunk who's only fit to do one thing and to tell you one thing. You are good, kind, hardworking doctors but you like me nevertheless and I know that you will allow me to tell you one thing—no, ask one thing—no, beg one thing of you. Please do this one favor for me, dear doctors. If you have a patient, young or old, suffering, dying, afflicted, useless, born or unborn whom you for the best of reasons wish to put out of his misery, I beg only one thing of you, dear doctors. Please send him to us, don't kill them—we'll take them, all of them. Please send them to us. I swear to you, you will not be sorry. We will all be happy about it. I promise you and I know you believe me, that we will take care of him, her—we will even call on you to help us take care of them—and you will not have to make such a decision. God will bless you for it and you will offend no one, except the great prince Satan who rules the world.

The mission of the faithful—those called to co-suffer with our fellow human beings—is summed up by this priest.

3

Suffering and Pain

YOU CANNOT LOVE WHAT shocks you. We must not respond to suffering with sentimental tenderness which, as O'Connor warns, when "detached from the person of Christ becomes death-dealing." What then is the response of the Word of God to suffering?

A good starting point is to differentiate suffering from pain. Pain is a real symptom that tells us something is wrong at the level of one's existence. Human beings exist on four levels: the physical, the psychological, the emotional, and the spiritual. Most of us understand physical, emotional, and psychological pain. But by spiritual pain I mean the experience that something is lacking in our sense of the self. One has lost touch with one's own identity.

That is spiritual pain. At all these levels, we feel as if we are sending out an S.O.S., a cry for help. Let us use a theological word. It is a cry for salvation. We want to be saved.

Suffering is the consciousness of pain, the kind of knowing that generates the question "why." This urge to ask why is in itself provocative. The Book of Job is one of our most dramatic examples of someone who needs to know why he is suffering and why all the explanations given to him are insufficient. If we ask why, it means that we have some idea of how it should be and something has occurred that doesn't fit that worldview. We ask why, therefore, in the light of an inexplicable imperfection that cannot be accounted for. Thus suffering makes us go beyond our preconceived worldview towards *something more*, and that's the first challenge — to try to find an answer in something more.

The question is a demand, a plea, that the perceived fault or imperfection of the self and the world be accessible to reason and rectified or at least answered. Actually, without this experience of imperfection, the notion of reason does not exist. Without suffering, we would never ask ourselves why. All would be immediately self-explanatory or evident.

In today's culture, everything must have an immediate explanation or be evident. If we believe this, then we cannot relate to suffering. We cannot relate to our own suffering or to someone else's suffering, unless we are willing to accept the question and to go beyond. Asking this question shows that we are convinced an answer is possible, that there is a higher schema of reason into which we want to be lifted so we can deal with this reality of suffering.

Therefore suffering — which includes this asking — is a sign of the conviction that there must be somewhere a source of reason that is always beyond our capacity to appreciate and to grasp within the moment. If not, we must settle for "that's just the way things are." The response to suffering cannot cut off the question.

Cry of the Heart

Suffering is a cry to God that characterizes the human person, and we do violence to the human person if we try to extinguish that cry. If we try to get rid of the pain in such a way that we would not be led to cry out, if there is no higher schema, if there is no God, it makes no sense to speak about suffering as suffering really is felt by human beings. All particular imperfections or pains are overshadowed by the universal one, which is death.

Suffering in the light of death is the great question, the great manifestation of human life, of the human person, of what distinguishes us and makes us human. Confronted with the phenomenon of our death or the death of a loved one, we cry out for an explanation. Existentially speaking, if there was no death, if we do not experience death as the ultimate pain, then life itself is without reason in itself but has whatever reason we arbitrarily give to it. If death is not respected, if it doesn't lead us to look for, to cry for, to ask for an answer, we are declaring ourselves the gods of life.

To deny death is to act like a god. Death reveals to us the existence of ultimate meaning, not by revealing to us its nature, but by compelling us to look for an answer. I believe that so many of the difficulties we have in understanding death arise because we don't want to search for that ultimate meaning. If death is no longer a problem, a mystery, then the suffering of the dying person becomes meaningless.

Or perhaps we are afraid to ask, afraid to go beyond?

And yet death is the inescapable fact of the life of each human being.

O'Connor said of Mary Anne, "She and the Sisters who had taught her had fashioned from her unfinished face the material of her death. The creative action of the Christian life is to prepare for his death in Christ. It is a continuous action in which this world's goods are utilized to the fullest, both positive gifts and what Père Teilhard de Chardin called passive diminishments."

"The creative action of the Christian's life is to prepare for his death in Christ." What gives our lives meaning is the sense we make of our own death and the death of loved ones — of those who are tied to our identity, because to be a human person is never an isolated experience. We always exist in terms of others, and it is our relationship to others that makes us someone. When loved ones suffer or die, our own suffering and death are occurring also. This is true even if that other person is someone we do not know, because, in the end, we are all united in our humanity. Therefore another's death is a challenge to us, because it anticipates our own death.

Protagonists in a Drama

In the light of that human solidarity, therefore, each of us sees that suffering and death are signs that I am not complete. Death and suffering cause us to question. And when we question, when we cry out in suffering for answers, we are crying out to God, to the source of ultimate meaning. Thus we enter into a dialogue with God. If we do this, it means that we believe that there is an author to our lives, a creator of humankind. We are not that author but protagonists in the author's play. Our task, therefore, is to understand the script. And yes, we must not only seek to understand but to love the play, the drama, and love our unique role in it—to be a protagonist, not just an extra in the drama of life.

This drama is written from beyond us. If there is no dramatic script, then all of life is improvisation, and we can walk off the stage any moment we want. If we're improvising, we are the author—in fact, there is no play, there are just billions of improvisations. But if there is an author who is not ourselves, if there is a script, we are the *dramatis personae* and know that the drama has an end we seek to understand. Suffering is that dialogue or questioning of God and of God seeking to make sense of the end of the drama of life. The question arises: Who am I in the light of this drama?

In St. Augustine's *Confessions*, he relates the impact he felt on the death of his friend. He wrote, "I became a great question or riddle or enigma to myself" (*Factus eram ipse mihi magna quaestio*). He meditates on his suffering and his questioning of God. I found it significant that he also questions his identity.

To suffer is not to be paralyzed by pain. On the contrary, it is to strain ahead, to walk on the basis of pain, to look towards a future. That is why suffering has a prophetic character. It is oriented beyond the self. If pain is absolutely abolished, the possibility of going beyond the self is eliminated. I think this is very important, because it's not just our pain in the light of our own death, but our pain in the light of someone we love. If we seek at all costs to abolish suffering, we cut off the possibility for questioning, for thinking, for straining forward and upward. Indeed, we must make every effort to reduce pain so that it not become paralyzing but can lead to that questioning, to a dialogue with God. That is the only proper context for human suffering. Without God, suffering is an abomination which must be eradicated.

Physical and psychological pain can be lessened, if not completely abolished, by medicine. This is a good thing. But when today's culture tries to abolish spiritual pain, it is abolishing the dialogue with God, the questioning that leads us beyond the self.

The Meaning of Spiritual Pain

How is spiritual pain abolished? It is abolished by utopias, by theories, by illusions, by idols, by lies, by false theologies that provide a kind of anesthesia for spiritual pain. "We are wrapped in theory," as O'Connor puts it, seeking to abolish spiritual pain so that it not lead to questioning, to suffering.

All the utopias, theories, illusions, idols, and false theologies are spiritually barren. What is fruitful, however, is when spiritual pain is directed to God as a prayer, as a plea—even as a demand, or a confession. Only then is there a possibility for a response to suffering. Only then is there a possibility for the redemption of suffering. This is the only response to suffering that does not deny reality or extinguish some crucial and important aspect of our life as persons.

Suffering is a cry for salvation, and the reply to it must be its redemption. Only God can grant it. We are not gods. We are not the authors of the script. To the degree that we believe that we are our own author, the notion of the redemption of suffering is meaningless. Without this insight into the redemption of suffering, we will stay at the level of the pain, be imprisoned by it. This is the death of our personhood. Everything will be directed to the negation of pain, all the way to the negation of natural death itself—in the form of euthanasia. If this happens, then we will be imprisoned in our refusal to look beyond the merely material, and we will lose the ability to grasp the reality of transcendence.

Our culture largely regards life as a sequence of mechanical functions, and therefore pain is understood as an error in a closed system—eliminating the drama of personal life that is oriented towards transcendence. Pain is merely something to be fixed. When we reflect on the relation between suffering and sin, we will see that contemporary culture sees sin as mistakes, errors in function, imperfections. This way of understanding humanity leaves no room for the drama of life. If there is a drama, there is an author, there is a script, suffering and redemption are experienced by understanding the drama and living it as an authentic protagonist.

To accept that we are protagonists in a cosmic drama is to break out of our material world and go beyond. This is a sign of our freedom. We will not settle for the notion that there is no meaning to life, that there is no drama, that we merely improvise. To believe that we are our own gods is an illusion, a denial of the reality of the existential meaning of life. But if we go beyond the material world for an answer to suffering, then we enter into a dialogue with the creator, and we are on the path towards transcendence.

This leads us to another concept: that of *co-suffering*. In his apostolic letter *Salvifici Doloris* on suffering, St. John Paul II talks about the "world" of suffering. There is a natural—if I may use the term—solidarity among sufferers. When someone co-suffers with us, then we become more and more persons—someones—walking towards transcendence together. Whoever does not recognize the fundamental solidarity of humankind, from which the desire to co-suffer with the other arises, is not fully human and remains an object, not a person. He or she is not free; he or she has become incapable of dialogue, because their life is a monologue with the self and not a dialogue with others and with God.

Treating someone as an object is a radical injustice. It is spiritual murder. The worst that can be done to someone else is to treat them like an object, a thing. Therefore, to do everything to avoid pain in order to deny suffering is to treat someone like an object. To take away the pain and the knowledge of suffering from someone is a radical injustice. Our response, in the light of that person's suffering, should be to join them in co-suffering. Only then will we affirm their fundamental humanity made in the image and likeness of God.

4

Suffering, Grace, Identity

I FIND MYSELF COMING BACK to that great phrase, "You cannot love what shocks you." Flannery O'Connor said the sisters in Atlanta "were shocked at nothing." If we are shocked by suffering, if we are repulsed, then we will try to eliminate it at all costs, including killing the person who suffers. We will justify this response by tenderness, the death-dealing tenderness which is, as she said, "wrapped in theory." Theory, in whatever shape it takes—whether philosophical, political, social, religious, or theological—is a great anesthetic that eliminates the spiritual pain upon which suffering—authentic human suffering—is concentrated.

The refusal to accept the challenge of suffering reflects our culture's allergy to transcendence.

Again, to paraphrase O'Connor, human imperfection is a sign of transcendence. It is a sign of the incompleteness of our lives on earth, an incompleteness at the very heart of what we are called to be and were created to be as human persons. Today's Western culture is incapable of dealing with personhood. As a result, the reality of the human person that points towards transcendence is negated by reducing the person to the level of an object (an object that can be manipulated). In this way, all suffering becomes merely a technical problem that requires fixing.

But we must not treat human beings as objects. That would mean that we have reduced the life of the person to a monologue—an improvised monologue that is meaningless. The true life of the human person is always a dialogue—a dialogue with someone else, with others. Human life is a drama because human freedom points towards the author of this drama, to a script not written by us and not written on earth. It's interesting that the Book of Job begins in heaven, where the drama that is about to unfurl is written. The relatively modern versions of that story—say in *Faust* by Goethe—also begin with a dialogue in heaven.

Suffering confronts us with the mystery of the transcendence of the person and their orientation to a spiritual reality that is not of this world.

Ironically, the existence of suffering has been used to discredit the existence of God. I propose that it is because there is a God that there is suffering. Suffering is a sign of God, a cry to the author of life. Our response to suffering must be to walk along with the sufferer towards God, to risk our own identity by relating with the one who suffers in his or her questioning. Often the one who is suffering is in a physical or mental state where he or she cannot question anything. Then we must question for them. In a mysterious sense, a solidarity is established between the sufferer and the co-sufferer. To be a co-sufferer is to involve one's personhood with the other, as the sufferer cries out to God. Authentic suffering, therefore, is a dialogue.

To co-suffer clearly doesn't mean to feel the pain of the other—but it is to share the existential questioning of the sufferer. To claim to feel the physical pain of the other is sentimentality; it is artificial tenderness. To co-suffer—to be a companion with the sufferer—is to walk alongside them towards transcendence. The one who does not co-suffer and is not prepared to do this cannot speak about it. Such a person does not know the truth and does not speak the truth. He or she is a liar—a deceiver, to use the words of Walker Percy. The task of someone confronted with the suffering of the other, especially people in the healthcare ministry, is to be willing to co-suffer. Co-suffering affirms the personhood of the sufferer and is an act of love. Co-suffering is the way we love the one who suffers.

The Symbolic Structure of Suffering

Suffering has a symbolic structure. Let me explain what that means. I use "symbol" in the original Greek meaning of the term. In the ancient world, a symbol was a half. If, for example, you were going to meet someone and you didn't know that person, you would cut a piece of ceramic in half—you keep one half and the other half is sent to that person (not unlike what they used to do in spy novels). Then, when you are going to establish that relationship, you whip out your half, and the other person brings out their half, and, if they match, the relationship is established.

That is a symbolic event—the word "symbol" indicates that. By saying that suffering has a symbolic structure, by saying that it unites persons, it brings them together in a particular enterprise, in the walk towards transcendence, towards the unknown, towards the mystery of the author of the drama that they are living as protagonists together. It unites in solidarity. It unites in dialogue.

What is the opposite of symbolic? It is diabolical. The inability to share that suffering, to co-suffer, to love—that is a diabolical reality. It separates, divides. I think Percy is right about our inability to respond to suffering by co-suffering. Even in the gospel, you will recall that when Jesus announced that he had to suffer and die, Peter resisted him. What did Jesus call him? He called him Satan. "You Satan," he said, "get away from me." You are not thinking like God. You don't want to walk along with me. Your response is to say: No, that cannot be. That cannot happen. You seek to destroy, to separate. You're not willing to co-suffer with me. You are Satan.

In this relationship with the one who suffers, the co-sufferer can impose nothing on the other. One can only help the other to ask—by asking together. This asking becomes more and more an act of prayer. The willingness to pray together with the one who suffers is the just response to the reality of suffering. Therefore, taking seriously that reality requires this co-praying.

The alternative is explanation, to constantly tell the other person: "this is what's happening. Sorry you don't see the answer, but it's very clear." Whatever answer you propose will partake of the false tenderness that seeks to eliminate suffering at all costs.

Since suffering has a prophetic character, to experience it is always to orient one's thought towards the future rather than the past. To look for an answer in the past is to reduce suffering to a functional problem that merely responds to causes in the past. Everything is explained in terms of causation. This approach to suffering does not do justice to the one who suffers; it is to reduce the one who suffers to an object—to deny the mystery, if you will, of human suffering.

The Secularization of Suffering

Of course, in a world that seeks to deny mystery, the result will be the secularization of suffering. We in the West live in a culture that cannot understand transcendence. Thus our culture seeks to eliminate suffering in ways that are inhuman. The mission of the Church—especially those engaged in the ministry of care for the suffering—is desperately needed to rescue the suffering person from manipulation as an object. Remember Job and his so-called friends? They would not co-suffer with him. They were theologians of the past. They tried to seek the origins of Job's suffering in the past, but he protested, repeatedly rejecting this method of understanding suffering. The empty and barren theology of Job's "comforters" is rejected by God himself at the end of the book.

We see the same tendency to explain away affliction in the case of the encounter between Jesus and the man born blind. The question is asked, "Why?" Is the man blind because of his sins or, perhaps, his parents' sins? Jesus says that it is not because of the past but because of the future. The blind man suffers this way so that God's glory may be manifest in him. The same can be said of Job and why he is not satisfied with the explanations of his "friends." His protest is a prayer.

Heidegger said that the pious man is not the one who recognizes himself as guilty before God when he suffers, but the one who struggles against God. Job struggled; Abraham struggled. The answer was sought not in terms of causes in the past, but in an expectation of the future — the future of which we are not the cause.

Thus the answer to suffering is always grace. Suffering is the call for the free grace that comes to us without conditions, without rationalizations, without explanations. Suffering can only be relieved by means of the co-sufferer helping the suffering person to have contact with that grace. The answer to suffering is always an experience of divine grace and love. To his so-called friends, Job was only the occasion for them to construct their own theology. They would not accept co-suffering with him, nor would they pray with him for grace. They had no knowledge of God's grace. Everything was fitted into a theological system that explained everything away.

Grace Bestows Identity

Grace is God's love. Grace is the sudden experience of the original love that created us and that makes us persons and that affirms that we are loved and worth everything, that we cannot and need not be reduced away to factors to justify our existence, that we are loved by God for ourselves. In other words, grace bestows identity.

This is one of the central themes of the teaching of Pope John Paul II. The human person is the only creature on earth that God created for its own sake. That is to say, we do not have to justify our existence because we have value in ourselves. Modern culture cannot understand this, especially when it is confronted with suffering. If we have no sense of the sanctity of the human person, then we cannot co-suffer. "The one who loves," St. Augustine said, "understands what I am talking about."

At the end of the Book of Job, it is significant that God doesn't give Job answers; instead, he begins to turn Job's mind to his identity, to remind him of who he is, that he is his creature. Job discovers that he is someone of such dignity that God does not even impose an answer on him but asks him questions. "Consider who you are." The Book of Job begins with a hint towards an asking and a reminder of who we are that surpasses anything we could have ever imagined. It ends with a hint of God somehow joining in that asking; therefore God, so to speak, is co-suffering with Job, praying with Job.

In one of his last essays, "Our Friends the Saints," the French novelist Georges Bernanos says:

> Right now, in our world, in some obscure Church or some old house or at the bend of a deserted road, there is some poor man who is joining his hands and from the depths of his misery, without really knowing what he is saying, or perhaps without saying anything at all, is thanking the good Lord for having made him free and capable of loving. Elsewhere, it doesn't matter where, there is a mother who is hiding her face for the last time against the little heart that no longer throbs, a mother, close to her dead child, offering God the moaning of an exhausted resignation, as if the Voice that threw the suns into the great void the way a hand disperses grain, the Voice that makes the earth tremble, had

46

just sweetly whispered in her ear: "Forgive me. One day you will know, you will understand, you will thank Me. But now, what I await from you is your pardon. Forgive Me." Those people—that harassed woman, that poor man—are at the heart of the mystery, at the core of universal creation and even inside the secret of God Himself.

Because it is there that we are going to penetrate and find the response—inside God himself. "What can I say of this," Bernanos goes on.

> Language is at the service of the intelligence. But what these people have grasped, they have understood by a faculty superior to the intelligence, though not at all in conflict with it, but at least it hasn't allowed explanations to take the problem away, or rather by a profound and irresistible impulse of the soul which engages all the faculties at the same time, which thoroughly absorbs all that is natural to them. . . . Truly, at the moment when that man and that woman accepted their destiny, they accepted themselves humbly.

Identity! This is what it means to be someone—to be a person. To accept this destiny. It is the greatest service we can render when we co-suffer with someone. In that experience, you are someone.

Bernanos concludes:

> The mystery of creation was accomplished in them while they were exposing themselves, without knowing it, to all the risks of human conduct; they fully realized themselves in the charity of Christ, themselves becoming, according to the words of St. Paul, other Christs.

Living in Solidarity

In John Paul II's apostolic letter on suffering, he says that it is in Colossians 1:24 that we discover the Christian response to suffering. When St. Paul says, "In my flesh I complete what is lacking in Christ's afflictions for the sake of His body that is the Church," he implies that he is co-suffering with Christ, that God's response to the suffering of the world, as the Book of Job suggests, is going to be in the form of a co-suffering with us. Paul is co-suffering with Christ on the cross, for others; but after suggesting that co-suffering is where we're going to find the ultimate disclosure of the truth about suffering, the Holy Father does a survey, not unlike what we have already done, about the phenomenon of suffering. Suffering, he says, is exclusively a human phenomenon; it is an expression of what man is. Only persons can suffer. Suffering, the pope says, points to man's transcendence. Suffering tells man to go beyond himself, not to settle for the past or the present, but to press on.

The Church, the Pope continues, is born out of the sufferings of Christ. She is, so to speak, the fruit of his sufferings, so she can and must meet man in the path of suffering. The Church has the mission to co-suffer with man, a mission that has many dimensions. It is through co-suffering with man that the Church encounters the human being. The mission of the Church is to so co-suffer with man so that each person can recognize himself or herself as a someone.

Suffering, he says, is revelatory. It discloses a great mystery that evokes fear and respect. When we face human suffering, we are awed. That is why some of the great

48

Christian saints have devoted their lives to the care of the suffering; the founders of these religious communities have found the Lord in the suffering person. We think of St. Francis kissing lepers, St. Jeanne Jugan picking up the old woman. The Holy Father says the light of faith begins to reflect on suffering. We see that behind suffering lies God. But at the heart of this mystery lies a great tragedy. Something has occurred. This tragedy goes beyond the suffering of this or that particular person. Those who suffer are caught up in a world of suffering, and we must see how we can live in solidarity with that world and see how God, out of tragedy, creates a new world of the redemption of suffering.

5

The Mystery of the Cross

WE SAW AT THE END of the Book of Job that it provided
no answer to Job's forceful questioning about his suffering.
Nor was Job answered by his friends, those theologians of
suffering. Instead, we are faced with the phenomenon of
God asking questions. I think that's important. In the end,
the problem of Job's suffering and all human suffering is
not responded to with definitive answers. Instead, it is
responded to by the risk of co-suffering, by entering into
the suffering of the sufferer, thus leading Job to reflect
on his own identity as well as God's identity. Job is led to
think of himself in terms of his relationship with God.

There is no theoretical answer to suffering. To
provide a theoretical answer—Job is being punished for
secret sins, for example—is an injustice to the sufferer.
Suffering is a mystery in the fullest sense of the word. It is
a mystery of faith. Human suffering, I propose to you, is
totally incomprehensible outside of the light of faith. No
worldly theory can adequately apprehend it, do it justice,
or do the sufferer justice and, therefore, provide insights

as to how to respond to it. It remains the question with which the greatest minds have struggled.

Suffering is always a scandal, an interruption, an irruption into our world of neat answers. Suffering leads us to break through into something much, much higher, something beyond us. It is a mystery because, as John Paul II says in his apostolic letter, it is exclusively a human phenomenon. It reveals what the human being is. Through suffering, our own suffering, or our experience of co-suffering with someone else, we touch the very heart of what it means to be a human being.

Suffering is revelatory of man. And, as John Paul II says, in particular, of man's transcendence as a person. It reveals man to be a person, and being a person is a mystery of faith. The concept of the person was born out of a struggle of the faith to understand the person of Christ. Therefore, suffering reveals the transcendence of man as a person, and by transcendence, I don't mean philosophical transcendence—that is to say, the fact that the human being goes beyond this world, beyond space and time. Rather, I mean that the human being is incomprehensible without Christ. The human being is a mystery of faith. Only faith can tell us who man is, because personal identity is related to the identity of the eternal Son of God.

The Revelation of the Incarnate Word

The Second Vatican Council, in its Constitution on the Church in the Modern World *Gaudium et Spes*, made the statement that has become a trademark of the teaching of John Paul II. It says, "Only in the mystery of the Incarnate Word is the mystery of man fully disclosed." These words have to be taken literally. No theory, no philosophy, no human science, can possibly grasp who the human person is outside of the light of faith in the Incarnate Word, in the God made Man. There exist partial explanations, of course, hence the phrase "fully understand." Without the light of faith, we can get hints, suggestions, and partial answers, but we cannot do man and woman full justice. I regret if this sounds triumphalistic or exclusivistic. Modern culture cannot understand the human person because it has rejected Christ. That is why it cannot confront suffering. It cannot deal with the Mystery of Christ.

Suffering reveals man's relationship to Christ. Remember Flannery O'Connor: detached from Christ, all that is left is theory, which soon leads to death-dealing tenderness. But attached to Christ, suffering provokes, as John Paul II also says in tandem with *Gaudium et Spes*, a great awe, a religious fear, because we are in the presence of the holy.

How is suffering a revelation of God and of the human person? We have been at the doorstep. Let us peek inside.

We have spoken of co-suffering as risking one's identity with the one who suffers by joining that person in the asking, in the praying, even when the prayer is a protest. That is an act of love, that is how we love the one who suffers. And if they are unable to question anymore, we question for them. This solidarity opens up what the Holy Father calls in the encyclical this experience of a "world of suffering." Our capacity to share the suffering without, as I said, experiencing the same pain or being in the same situation, leads to an experience of suffering as a world. This is a crucial insight.

The world of suffering reveals that all suffering is related, that something is wrong that goes beyond any one particular manifestation of suffering. The Holy Father says that "suffering introduces into the reality of evil something of a mysterious magnitude…. There is a great wound in the heart of human existence." That is part of what he means by the experience of the world of suffering.

The True Nature of Sin

The Catholic faith tells us that suffering is tied to sin. But what is sin? We confront again another mystery, because it has to do with our relationship, our identity with Christ. Without Christ, we cannot even know sin. Without the insight of faith into our own identity's relationship to his identity, we cannot grasp the horror of sin, and, therefore, we do not understand the nature of evil. Thus, we cannot understand suffering.

Our experience, thought, theology, and philosophy propose all kinds of answers to the problem of guilt, punishment, suffering as punishment, the problem of the justice of God. But these answers are, at best, partial and misleading, even dangerous, since they lead many to see suffering as a punishment for the sin of the sufferer. And we know how Christ rejected this explanation in his encounter with the blind man, how Job rejected this explanation from his "comforters."

Suffering is, as the experience of the world of suffering shows, related to evil and sin, but Jesus says that it is also revelatory of God's glory. The danger of this statement was experienced by St. Paul, who was constantly misunderstood for claiming this. Where sin exists, grace abounds. In the end, suffering and its relation to sin should lead us to reflect on God's glory. And how can one describe this idea? God's glory is the inexpressible beauty of God, it is the overwhelming ecstasy that is the experience of God's boundless love—a love that is totally unconditional, boundless, infinite grace. Our point of entrance, Jesus suggests, to an experience of God's glory is suffering. If the sufferings of the man born blind had led us to a display of God's glory, then we should see all suffering as revelatory of the glory of God.

Only in the light of the cross can we understand this shocking statement. Like St. Paul, we offer the revelation of Christ crucified as the revelation of the glory of God and of the unsurpassable dignity of the human person called to share ecstatically in that glory.

We have seen hints of how we may understand this in the act of co-suffering, especially in the love that is willing to risk one's identity as a person in the face of the suffering of someone else in order to affirm their identity. When we take on the questioning of the sufferer, we risk our identity with them. We lend them our identity and so join with them in an inexpressible union that reaches down into the deepest part of the self.

The Restoration of Identity

In the end, however, our identity is not strong enough to totally restore the identity of the one who suffers. Human love by itself is confronted with death. But what

if the co-sufferer is the author of our identity? This is
the mystery of the cross. Then Christ's co-suffering is
enough. "My grace is sufficient for you, for my power is
made perfect in weakness" (2 Corinthians 2:19). Only he
can totally heal the personal diminishment, the spiritual
pain; only he can redeem suffering.

The identity of the one who is on the cross directs
our attention to the magnitude of the problem behind the
mystery of suffering. It is indeed related to the mystery of
sin, to a fate that has befallen humanity. We only know
the magnitude of sin in the light of what its redemption
cost. The cross reveals that sin is a reality that has struck at
the heart of God's creation and the relationship between
the divine and the human. If sin requires the cross for the
revelation of its magnitude and for its elimination, then it
must be something much more than a matter of injustice
or an offense towards God, something that has altered
more than a judicial relationship between the offender
and the offended. What is happening on the cross must
be much more than a revelation that God sides with those
who are suffering. I would say that even seeing the cross as
the means for forgiveness of sins is insufficient.

In short, I think those who protest their suffering
like Job are in the right. Jesus didn't die because this world
is cruel and good people suffer. He died because, through
His death, God is redeeming suffering. God is restoring
personal identity. He—the someone on that cross—is
sharing his identity with us. To share identity means that
there is a bond between us that must have been present
from the very beginning. My concern is that we tend to
see the event of the cross and its application to us in an

external way, as merely a judicial payment of a debt that somehow or other we don't have to pay.

But the mystery of the cross is much deeper than this: there is a link between us and Christ from the very beginning of our existence. This is what I mean when I say that the human person cannot be understood without Christ. What is happening on the cross is an affirmation of the identification of Christ and humanity in the face of sin and death, an affirmation which is the fruit of God's boundless love and glory. This link is stronger than sin and stronger than death. Therefore, no amount of sin and suffering can ever diminish the infinite dignity of the human person. The human person is created to be an expression, an image of God the Father's eternal Son. The love between the Father and the Son is to be extended to this creature we know as the human person. That is the source of the dignity of every human person.

The Trinitarian Mystery

In a bold statement, the Second Vatican Council says that from the very beginning of a man or a woman's existence in the womb of their mother, he or she is in relationship with Christ. Such is the ineffable dignity of the human person. In an unforgettable address at the end of the Second Vatican Council, Pope Paul VI spoke of the confrontation between the humanism that faith in Christ leads us to and the humanism that's triumphant in the modern world without Christ, without God. He says the two have faced each other in the Council, and he makes a plea to secular humanists who are honestly searching for answers: "I hope that you will at least grant us this, that we more than you worship man."

It is interesting to note that, in the official publication of the speech, the phrase "worship man" was changed to "honor man." That was not what the pope said. We worship man because man is inseparably tied to Christ. Human identity is to share in the identity of the eternal Son of the living God, who is love. No merely human thought system can reach this insight. Those who try and know that something is lacking are forced to conclude, correctly, that, without this insight, personal life is a tragedy. Without Christ, we might as well not exist. It is because we do not know Christ that we despair of our existence. That is why suicide can have a terrifying appeal. The cross tells us who we were meant to be from the beginning. It shows us what has occurred and how God has responded to it and how we too can respond to it.

The Resurrection tells us the end of the drama, of the triumph of divine love and, with it, the triumph of human identity linked with the identity of Christ. Because Christ shared our suffering to the end, even unto death and beyond, to whatever the mystery of the descent into hell means. This is only possible if we say that God is love, if we believe that there is a Father and a Son and a Spirit. No other doctrine but that of a Trinitarian God can address the problem of human identity and, therefore, the problem of suffering. To repeat, our existence as persons is the direct result of there being a Trinitarian God. We exist as persons in Christ. This is the biblical concept of creation in Christ.

We exist as persons because of the Father's desire to extend his love for his Son to a creature like us. Our identity, therefore, is inseparable from this love between the Father and the Son. It's inseparable from Christ's identity. The Trinitarian fatherhood of God is extended to the world in Jesus. God wants to be the same good for the world that He is in Himself and for Himself—namely, a Trinitarian communion of love. Man and woman are created out of this overwhelming glory of God's love and, because of this, can only find their final fulfillment through a participation in divine love.

The Redemption of Suffering

It is against this common identity with Christ that sin strikes. When sin strikes, the very identity of Christ is at stake, the very reality of the Trinity. This is its horror. When sin strikes, John Paul II says in the encyclical on divine mercy, reflecting on the parable of the prodigal son, the fatherhood of God is diminished. That is a bold statement, and it shows that our very existence is tied to the fate of the Trinitarian God.

That is why sin and its consequences can only be overcome by the affirmation that the Son's identity, and ours in him, is stronger than sin and its consequence of suffering and death. Thus the Son enters the world of suffering and death in order to co-suffer with us and restore our identity as persons. Sin contradicts the Trinitarian fatherhood of God, but the cross restores it because of the One suffering and dying. Sin rejects God not as creator, but as father. The suffering and the death of the One on the cross who is the eternal Son is an affirmation of the boundless love of God and of the infinite dignity of the human person. Sin and its consequences intend the separation between the Father and the Son. The cross shows that this separation is impossible, and so it renders sin powerless. That is why we should not be shocked by suffering, because in it we can come to know God's love through our faith in the mystery of the sufferings of Jesus Christ. If we do not believe this, we will be shocked by suffering; we will despair and seek to eliminate the sufferer or ourselves.

The redemption of suffering is not merely an answer to suffering but an event that restores our identity. The identity of the most miserable, wretched person on earth is defended by the identity of the eternal Son and the price he paid for it.

Our response to suffering can only be with Christ, to co-suffer and enter from the world of suffering into the world of redemption and bring ourselves and the one with whom we suffer into this redemption. We can only do this because we have been granted a share in the mission of Christ.

6

To Complete What Is Lacking

THE MYSTERY OF HUMAN suffering is a revelation of the mystery of Christ and his identity and of our human identity tied to his from the very beginning of our existence. The world of suffering is the result of the tragedy that occurred when the first Adam betrayed this identity under the suggestion of the Great Deceiver. The second Adam — to use Pauline terms — has introduced us to a new world, the world of the redemption of suffering.

Just as suffering is a communal reality, the concept of a world of suffering is the only way to understand the suffering of the innocent. If suffering is communal, it follows that the redemption of suffering itself is communal. It is through co-suffering with or in Christ that the word of God and the power of God's love encounters the reality of human suffering.

It is important to state that redemption does not eliminate suffering, and to eliminate it by our own actions is an injustice. Redemption changes the meaning of suffering from an occasion of diminishment to an occasion of the affirmation of one's unsurpassable dignity tied to the dignity of Jesus Christ himself and, in Him, to the glory of God who is a love stronger than sin, stronger than death.

The world of suffering is a world of efficacious co-suffering in Christ who provides a space for us to join him in his co-suffering mission. Redemption is a mission that we share with Him, though it is entirely dependent on Him. By ourselves, we do not have the power to redeem suffering. Only in Him do we have that power. Redemption is not automatic—it is contingent on human freedom. Redemption is an invitation to a free response on our part, an invitation to accept walking with Christ with a new identity, a new vocation, a new mission. Redemption is being confronted with the cross and suddenly realizing that we must respond and take it up just as Simon of Cyrene took up the cross.

The Secret of Suffering

It is precisely this co-suffering with Christ that has salvific value for others. If we walk along with Him who redeems suffering, then others will experience a relief in suffering. By this I mean the human ability to affirm the identity of the one who suffers by sharing God's love in and for Christ with them. This I believe is Paul's experience in that passage from Colossians 1:24 that John Paul II in *Salvifici Doloris* calls not the solution to suffering (because suffering is a mystery, not a problem to be solved) but the discovery—even the joyful discovery—of the secret of suffering. That is, in our own flesh we complete what is lacking in Christ's afflictions for the sake of His body, the Church. John Paul II says this represents the final discovery at the end of the drama of salvation history, that we are co-sufferers with Christ in whom the world of suffering is redeemed.

How do we understand Paul's experience? It is important for us to remember that we are speaking of the redemption, the restoration of personal life, and that life is always communal. We are only persons in relationship with another by saying yes to the love of another. The creative love behind the world of persons is the love between the Father and the Son. It is this love that gives us our identity, and we become persons by saying yes to this divine love, by saying yes to the invitation to share the life, the identity of Jesus Christ. The redemption of suffering—the restoration of the individual person who has been wounded by sin—also requires this yes, the willingness to share in the sufferings of Christ and open ourselves up to what His cross reveals.

The model for this yes is given in the yes of Mary, the Mother of Jesus. She is the essential part of any understanding of her Son. She is the path to discovering the reality of the truth about redemptive suffering, both her own and her Son's on the Cross.

In short, we must make ours the yes of Mary. Out of this assent is born the Church, the communion of co-sufferers with Christ, the glory of redeemed humanity. Therefore, the redemption of suffering has the form of allowing for co-suffering with Christ. This is the secret of true compassion: it is compassion with the Passion. It is the space in which the Christian church—the communion of believers—lives. Any attempt by the Church to leave this space, to separate ourselves from an existence which is that of co-suffering with Christ, is a betrayal of the cross.

No Longer I but Christ

This truth is kept present in our world through the Eucharist, through which we join with the body of Christ. In this way, the world of suffering as well as our wounded identities are mystically restored in Christ Jesus through the entrance into a new world, a new creation. The whole Church, the whole Body of Christ, must be co-crucified with her Head in the sharing of the Father's love for the Son, the sharing of the Son's identity, so that we can look at the cross and say, "There we hang." There is where we place ourselves. We have no other self but Christ's. Who we are as persons hangs on that cross and is sustained by the love of the Father for Jesus. This is the only thing that gives us our identity and dignity.

This is another experience of Paul that he refers to in Galatians 2:19-20: "It is no longer I who live but Christ who lives in me." This is the Church's being—to co-suffer with Christ. This is her mission, her identity, especially when she approaches the sick and the suffering. Who else can approach them this way? The secular world is shocked because for them, as St. Paul says, the cross is a scandal. Since suffering is a revelation of Christ on the cross, without an acceptance of the cross, without an acceptance of being on the cross with Jesus, we will find suffering an abomination that must be eliminated at all costs. For, as Flannery O'Connor says: "You cannot love what shocks you."

The great theologian Hans Urs von Balthasar expresses it this way in a wonderful book called *The Moment of Christian Witness*:

> Everything that I am (insofar as I am anything
> more on this earth than a fugitive figure without
> hope, all of whose illusions are rendered worthless
> by death), I am solely by virtue of Christ's death,
> which opens up to me the possibility of fulfillment
> in God. I blossom on the grave of God who died for
> me. I sink my roots deep into the nourishing soil of
> his flesh and blood. The love which I draw in faith
> from this soil can be of no other kind than the love
> of the one who is buried.

The consequence of this in the midst of suffering is the ability to say, "not I suffer, but Christ in me." Christ has created for Himself in me an organ for his redemption so that we should not carry our suffering (which no longer exists), but we carry, as St. Paul says in 2 Corinthians 4:10, the dying of Jesus in our bodies in order that the life of Jesus may be manifested in our mortal flesh.

In the Christian experience, one's suffering is a loan, a loan by which, through consent, one remains indebted to the true owner. (Which is why the desire to eliminate suffering at all costs is to refuse this responsibility for the gracious loan given to us.) The authentic human solidarity of Jesus as the second Adam—the truth of our identity shared with him before the Father, which is the only way it can be found, restored, defended—is what creates the truth of co-suffering with him, of completing his sufferings.

Saying Yes to the Cross

Of course, we add nothing to the sufferings of Christ. By completing his suffering, we say the yes that is required because we are free persons, the yes that is required for his sufferings to be redemptive in me. No one can say that yes for me. My identity in Christ is offered to my freedom. My freedom must be involved in redemption. Through this yes, I consent to live incorporated in Christ crucified and risen. My yes to the sacraments of the Church — to Baptism, to the Eucharist, the sacrament of Penance — is a yes to this desire, a yes to this recognition of my identity as that of the One on the cross. To live that posture of yes to the cross is the fullest expression of who Christ is. In so doing, I prove that the sufferings of Christ are redemptive.

To refuse to live this way is, as St. Paul says, to nullify the grace of God, to declare that he has died in vain. My identity, who I am, had been removed by sin from the design of the Father. Only by saying yes to the cross, by freely placing myself there, can I manifest Christ as Lord, as the One in whom my identity is grounded.

Moreover, to co-suffer with someone is to stake our identity on the cross of Christ with that person. In this way, we experience on the cross the affirming love of the Father, along with the someone who is either asking, pressing on, protesting, surrendering, or who may be incapable of anything at all. If we accept that person, if we decide freely to co-suffer with that person, if we stake our identity on the cross with that person, if we love that person with the love of Christ, then we are restoring and affirming their identity, their dignity — we are relieving their suffering.

This is the mystery of the redemption of suffering. It is here that we can see the relevance of this truth to the future of Catholic healthcare, which is based on the recapturing of this vision and on a recommitment to this dedication without embarrassment—otherwise the entire system is a sham. Catholic healthcare institutions and communities must be agents of Christ's love and of the Father's love for his Son on the cross—or else Catholic healthcare deserves no future. Catholic health institutions must be homes where those who suffer find their identity, where their identity is restored by the power of Christ's love. These hospitals, hospices, and health facilities must be places where the sufferer encounters respect and relief.

Von Balthasar says the glory of God—the inexpressible beauty of that glory that is His love—strikes human beings, stamps them, shapes them, so that their lives become what von Balthasar calls a "style of life," a particular way of manifesting what God's glory is like. The saints have shown different styles, and there are as many styles as there are people, because the glory of God is inexhaustible, and each one of us is someone irreplaceable before God.

The Example of Padre Pio

The style that led me to this thinking is the style of a humble Italian Capuchin monk, the priest known as Padre Pio of Pietrelcina. He was born in 1899 and died in 1968 and bore the stigmata. In 1956, this Italian Capuchin priest-monk with no resources built a hospital in the middle of rocky mountains in the southern part of Italy. He did not call it a hospital. He called it "The Home for the Relief of Suffering." It is a vast complex on top of the hill next to the small church where he is buried and the monastery where he lived.

As a hospital, the scientific-technical care provided there is incomparable—on the cutting edge of all the advances in modern medicine. It has a nursing school, a medical school, and a nurse aide training school. It has nursing homes and homes for people who are handicapped. It has everything. What is remarkable is that all of this is from a man who just stayed in that little monastery. Said Mass, heard confessions, and was bleeding from the stigmata all the time.

I tried to understand that. I asked myself: What is the secret of this place? The answer: This place is borne out of St. Pio's co-suffering with Christ, a co-suffering dramatized in a marvelous way by the phenomenon of the stigmata, the symbol of the love between the Father and the Son on the cross. This reminded me of St. Paul: "I carried in my body the dying of Jesus, so that the life of Jesus may be manifested." And I saw how Padre Pio carried in his body the dying of Jesus, especially when he celebrated the Eucharist. Padre Pio was totally devoted to the Sacrament of Penance and therefore knew the mystery of the forgiveness of sins, which is not just a judicial transaction, but a restoration of dignity and identity.

This holy man grasped the final discovery of what John Paul II said about the meaning of Paul's words on sharing in Christ's suffering, as evidenced by the fruit of that home for the relief of suffering. I was attracted to this because Padre Pio personally did not establish a religious congregation for the care of the sick. He just prayed, suffered, said the Mass, and heard confessions. Padre Pio's "style" of co-suffering with Christ based on the Eucharist and Penance—the heart of his identity as a priest—led to the relief of suffering. This must be the "style" or charism of all authentic Catholic healthcare, or else it is a sham.

Padre Pio said to those involved in healthcare:

> You have the mission to look after the sick, but if to the sick bed you do not bring love, I don't believe that medicines will help much. How could you express love if not through words which bring spiritual relief to the sick person. Bring God to the sick. It will be worth more than any other cure. In the sick person there is Jesus who is suffering. In the poor, sick person there is Jesus Christ. We should complete the formation of this hospital so it may become a temple of prayer and of science where the human race may find itself as one flock under one Shepherd in Jesus crucified. This work, if it were only for the relief of bodies would amount to a model clinic built by the means of your charity which has been extraordinarily generous, but this has been stimulated and encouraged to be an active reminder of the love of God through the call to charity. The one who is suffering should live in this hospital, experiencing the love of God by means of the wise acceptance of his sufferings, by the serene meditation of his destiny in Him on the cross. In this home the love of God should strengthen the spirit of those who are sick by means of love for Jesus crucified which will radiate out from those who assist the infirmity of His body and of His spirit. Here patients, doctors, and priests will be reservoirs of love which will be more abundant inasmuch as it will be shared with the others. The priest and the doctors bound together in their exercise of charity towards those who are sick in body will feel the burning stimulus of remaining too in the love of God so that both they and those

whom they are assisting may have a single dwelling
place in Him with life and love.

The love of the Spirit, the love that led Padre Pio
to spiritualize the endeavors and mission of Catholic
healthcare, provides an unparalleled example for the
future of Catholic healthcare. The Church in this world is
eccentric and must accept that fate because her Lord was
an outcast. Padre Pio echoes Walker Percy's outcast priest
in *The Thanatos Syndrome* when he says:

> If you have a patient, young or old, suffering,
> dying, afflicted, useless, born or unborn whom you
> for the best of reasons wish to put out of his misery,
> I beg only one thing of you, dear doctors. Please
> send him to us, don't kill them—we'll take them,
> all of them. Please send them to us. I swear to you,
> you will not be sorry. We will all be happy about
> it. I promise you and I know you believe me, that
> we will take care of him, her—we will even call on
> you to help us take care of them—and you will not
> have to make such a decision. God will bless you
> for it and you will offend no one, except the great
> prince Satan who rules the world.

How is such divine wisdom (the wisdom of St.
Pio and Percy's fictional priest), this presence of Christ,
received in one's heart? Only by following Christ always,
by traveling the way of the cross of Christ that leads to
wisdom and true life, exposing the great error of those
who think themselves wise by their own efforts. "Come
to me, all of you who are tired and overburdened," He
said—you whose search for wisdom has been futile,
unable to satisfy the desires of your heart. Padre Pio came
to Him, gave himself entirely to Him, and thus became

the way for millions who followed Christ with him and in him. Padre Pio personified the following of Christ as St. Paul described it in his letter to the Galatians: "As for me, I bear in my body the very signs of Christ."

This is what matters in life. This is the secret of love, the secret of life, making of us apostles for the relief of suffering in a world so desperately in need of love.

Lorenzo Albacete

A Short Biography

John Touhey

IF LORENZO ALBACETE'S REFLECTIONS on suffering seem especially perceptive, it is with good reason—he knew the material thoroughly from hard-won personal experience. Born in San Juan, Puerto Rico in 1941 to a family proud of its Spanish and Latin American roots and observant of the Catholic traditions that suffused the culture of their island, Lorenzo's early life was full of joy and laughter. He was handsome, smart, funny—and popular with his peers. His empathy and loyalty made him an ideal friend. From a young age, however, Lorenzo also faced trials that would reverberate throughout the course of his life, beginning with the illness of his younger brother Manuel.

"I was an only son for many years, until my brother came along and ruined it all," Albacete once quipped. In actual fact, then six-year-old Lorenzo greeted the arrival of Manuel with great enthusiasm. In an old photograph, he beams as he holds his baby brother on his lap. The boys were a close-knit pair from the start but grew even more attached when it became evident that Manuel suffered from psychological problems that would eventually be diagnosed as obsessive-compulsive disorder with borderline schizophrenia.

The severity of Manuel's illness meant that certain social interactions were deeply challenging for him. Despite his sharp and inquisitive mind, Manuel struggled in school. Lorenzo became his younger brother's helpmate and protector, aiding him with his homework, encouraging him in the many moments that he was overcome by fear, and constantly making jokes to ease his mind and spirit. For his part, Manuel came to rely increasingly upon his older brother for support and would, over time, grow jealous of Lorenzo's gregariousness and the public attention he received. As with many sibling relationships, theirs was a complicated dynamic, intensified by the unique circumstances they would endure over the following six decades.

Even with Manuel's struggles, the early years of the Albacete brothers always held an idyllic place in their memories. Their father, the elder Lorenzo, had married relatively late in life. Never expecting to have children, he shamelessly spoiled his sons beyond his humble means. Their mother, Conchita Cintrón, was a beautiful, affectionate woman with an eccentric wit—a characteristic that she would pass on to her eldest son. She and Lorenzo both enjoyed a good joke and to dress up and strike poses for the camera. Laughter was common in the Albacete household. They were not a rich family, but they were happy.

In 1956, Lorenzo and Manuel lost their father unexpectedly. His death was a blow to both boys but was felt with particular keenness by Manuel, who had relied on his father as an emotional anchor. Conchita Albacete simply shut down. Whenever a visitor knocked at the door, she would grab her sons and cower behind the furniture. For all the love she showed them and her many gifts, Conchita lacked the emotional fortitude and the practical skills needed to navigate the difficult years that followed her husband's death.

As the years unfolded, the younger Lorenzo became increasingly responsible for his family's future, not just financially but emotionally and in the mundane demands of daily life. Whether due to a tic of his personality or some deeper inner struggle, Lorenzo Albacete never felt that he could adequately bear this burden. Though he would master calculus and orbital mechanics, paying bills on time and organizing calendars seemed beyond his abilities. Perhaps these simple tasks were uninteresting to him— or it may be that it is here that we find the seeds of a self-awareness that would develop in the coming years, as the brilliant youth began to understand and come to terms with his own incapacities and his need for a mercy that surpassed human limits. Whatever the case, one of Conchita's sisters fortunately stepped in to manage their affairs and keep the family functioning.

It was an emotional parting when Lorenzo boarded a plane in the late 1950s to attend Catholic University in Washington, DC. There he studied aeronautical engineering and went on to earn a master's degree in aerospace physics. While working towards his doctorate, he was employed at the Naval Ordnance Laboratory in White Oak, Maryland as a researcher. Much of the work he did in this period was classified. That made it impossible to complete his thesis, but when he realized this, it no longer mattered: "I had already recognized my vocation to the priesthood."

The call to the priesthood came to Lorenzo directly, during a papal trip to Bogota, Columbia, in 1968. Manuel, who was then working at a travel agency, had arranged the trip for his brother. Hoping to get closer to Pope Paul VI, Lorenzo dressed up in priestly attire and joined a group of clergy. According to Cardinal Seán O'Malley (then a young Capuchin friar, who had become close friends with Lorenzo at this time), Lorenzo recounted the punchline of the story: "When he confessed to the pope he was not really a priest, Saint Paul VI said: 'Why don't you become a priest?'"

The pope's proposal took root, but the soil had already been prepared. During his years of study and work, Lorenzo began to conceive of human existence in a new way — informed by an experience of "another land," as he called it. Just a few months before his encounter with Paul VI, he had written about this new land in a letter to his infant godson on the occasion of his baptism:

> It takes so long at times … to begin to understand the laws of life of this other world, to breathe its air, to see its signs. Today you have, as it were, been given new eyes, new ears, new hands, a new tongue, even a new nose. Now you must learn to use them. To see, to hear, to touch, to smell, to talk about this new life which is infused throughout the other: like the seawater which wets the shore and goes temporarily away, like the breeze which moves the leaves on the trees in Rock Creek Park.

If you do not use these new senses, they will atrophy, they will surely die. If this happens, you will see nothing, you will not hear the sounds of life, you will detect no sweet fragrance, you will extend your hands and touch no one, your talk will be in vain.

But if you do develop your new senses, you will come into contact with life (after perhaps a painful and bitter struggle, but a pain that becomes joy, a struggle that leads to victory and peace); if you do read the signs of Its presence amongst men, then your eyes will see beauty, you will hear music, your touch will be soft, you will grasp at times an incomparable fragrance, your talk will be wisdom.

A year later, Lorenzo Albacete, "with trepidation" but having "experienced a profound call to follow without reservations or conditions," ended a relationship with a woman he was expecting to marry in order to enter the seminary. He was 28. Lorenzo studied for the priesthood at Washington's Theological College, run by the Sulpician order, which at the time was known for its progressive views. Since the release of the encyclical *Humanae Vitae* by Pope Paul VI, there had been turmoil within the Church not just about the morality of birth control but about the general relationship of faith to the secular world. The Catholic Church had seemingly divided into two camps in the years after the Second Vatican Council which would, unhelpfully, become associated with the political labels of "right" and "left." When he arrived at the seminary, Lorenzo Albacete had already found both sides inadequate. Even while he was engaged in his scientific research, Lorenzo was volunteering as a staff writer for the monthly magazine *Triumph*, known for mercilessly lampooning adherents of modernism in the Church while simultaneously sounding off against the excesses of capitalism and opposing the war in Vietnam.

Unlike his fellow seminarians, Lorenzo would speak up whenever a professor presented a dubious argument in class. His rebuttals, usually in defense of some Church teaching, were delivered with perspicuity and an often devastating humor that riled many of the faculty. Lorenzo, who had been personally placed in the seminary by Cardinal Patrick O'Boyle, the Archbishop of Washington, felt free to keep expressing his views regardless of the outcry. According to Fr. Francis Early, a friend of Albacete's from this period:

> Lorenzo told me he was called in one day by the rector with a complaint from the teachers, because he was challenging what they were teaching and debating them in class in front of the other students—and Lorenzo was winning, I think. So the rector said, "If I have one more complaint about you, you're out, I'm expelling you from the seminary." And Lorenzo said to the rector, "Oh, thank you. I hope you do. You will be doing me a favor because Cardinal O'Boyle told me if I was expelled from TC, it would be a sign to him from God that he was to ordain me immediately." He said the rector then never threatened him again with expulsion.

Soon after his ordination, it became clear that Fr. Lorenzo Albacete would be a different kind of priest. The first time he served "night duty" at his new parish, he answered a phone call from a distraught woman who said that her sister had just been killed in a plane crash. Fr.

Lorenzo brought her coffee and donuts, and the two of them sat mourning in the kitchenette of her apartment.

Two weeks later, he heard his first confession. The penitent had entered his confessional on a whim, telling Fr. Lorenzo that he had been heading to McDonald's. "I hope you don't want a Big Mac with french fries," said Fr. Lorenzo, "because if so, you have made a grave mistake." The man chuckled, then warned Fr. Lorenzo that he was about to tell him "things that you have never heard in confession before." Fr. Lorenzo assured him that would not be hard: "This is my first confession. Anything you say will be a shock to me." The man burst out laughing. Recalling the moment decades later, Albacete said that the parishioners who had been waiting to confess to him "fled to the other confession line."

William Baum, who succeeded O'Boyle as Archbishop of Washington, made Lorenzo Albacete his Secretary for Theological Research. He later served in a similar role under Baum's successor Cardinal James Hickey. Fr. Lorenzo also did advisory work for the National Conference of Catholic Bishops and the Holy See. These activities were welcomed by Albacete, not just because they put his talents to use in the service of the Church, but also because he needed the extra money. By this time his mother and brother had moved to Silver Spring, Maryland, in close proximity to the various parishes where Lorenzo served as a resident priest over the next several years. In addition to his work for his bishops, Fr. Lorenzo carried out his sacramental duties — celebrating Mass, hearing confessions, performing baptisms, preaching. He was also responsible for ministering to the local Hispanic community. The rest of Fr. Lorenzo's time was devoted to caring for his family. Manuel was still working, but his salary did not cover his and his mother's many expenses, so Lorenzo picked up some extra income as a counselor and lecturer at the Inter-American Development Bank in the city.

It made for an exhausting routine. A spiritual journal that Fr. Lorenzo kept during this period reflects the struggles he faced—personal, familial, and as a priest in a Church that was also being tested by circumstances. As he wrote: "I think of all that has happened to my family.... It is devastating, literally. And to the country, the Church. We are tired, exhausted, beaten, unable to communicate." His journal entries show just how entwined his family life was with his priestly vocation. They also reveal a man who experienced a deep familiarity with God:

> Saturday, June 11, 1977: Give me more, more of your grace and strength. My garden just has little puddles of water.

On Tuesday, June 14, the day before his brother was to see a psychiatrist, Fr. Lorenzo wrote:

> Manuel is having an attack of nerves as I write this. It is all because of tomorrow. Astounding! What can be done? What are your plans, Lord? What is a spiritual life like under these circumstances? What must I do?

> Wednesday June 15: What a marvelous thing it is when you display your power and grant us peace. I am thinking of Manuel today....

> Thursday, June 16: Scared a little bit about Mami today, but only a moment. What could I do tomorrow to celebrate Sacred Heart? My brother asks me to beg you to give him (and us) a good day

in earthly ways! It really takes a lot of love in your heart to accept our stupidity. I shall be bold [and] ask you for it.

Sunday, June 19: Yesterday, my brother really "celebrated" the Mass. I would not have done it if he had not insisted! Please accept his spiritual sacrifice; he who is so much a victim. Purify it and make it acceptable and bountiful in peace and health.

Wednesday, June 22: Being under the shadow of your wings could be confused with darkness. You have big wings....

His sense of inner tumult is still apparent a few weeks later, on July 13:

Why this feeling of walking next to a precipice? What lack of trust! You really must—well, let's say, would—get tired of me if you were not God!

The day's entry ends, as many do, in a single word: "Mercy."

†

Almost a year before recording his pleas to God, Albacete had an encounter that would eventually alter the course of his life and priesthood, though he did not realize it at the time. Karol Wojtyla, the Cardinal of Krakow, Poland, visited Washington for three days, and Albacete was asked by Cardinal Baum to look after him. Wojtyla and Albacete quickly established a rapport, realizing that they shared many of the same interests and concerns. Mostly, Albacete was impressed by Wojtyla himself. Here was a figure who had experienced persecutions under the Nazis and Communists, a poet and dramatist, an avid skier and mountain climber who had just led the Lenten retreat for Pope Paul VI and his household. He was, in short, "a Man with a capital M," as Albacete later recalled. When he dropped Cardinal Wojtyla off at the airport, they agreed that Albacete would read certain texts that the Cardinal suggested and that they would stay in touch by letter. Wojtyla did send Albacete letters, but they were left unanswered.

When Karol Wojtyla was elected Pope John Paul II in 1978, Fr. Lorenzo was flabbergasted. "This is awful!" a friend recalls him exclaiming, panicked by the thought that he had disappointed a man he not only admired but who was now his boss. Pope John Paul II did not let him off the hook. When Lorenzo went to Rome a month later, the pope fixed him with his gaze in the receiving line and told him, "Well, Lorenzo, I guess you'll answer my letters now!"

Lorenzo Albacete would never neglect their friendship again. Rather, he became an expert in John Paul II's theology, writing his doctoral dissertation on his teaching. His time studying in Rome, during which he also worked for Cardinal Baum at the Congregation for Catholic Education, was a period of relative security and peace. Photographs from this time show Lorenzo at a private audience in the Vatican, presenting his mother and brother to the pope. (They had met briefly once before during a papal visit to Washington.) Conchita and Manuel wear awed smiles, and Lorenzo looks very at ease and cheerful with his friend who also happens to be the Supreme Pontiff.

During this period, Fr. Lorenzo encountered several fellow sojourners who were also fascinated by John Paul II's thought and, in particular, by his complex and fascinating discourses on human sexuality and marital love, which he called the Theology of the Body. To engage these and other questions that touched upon the depth and mystery of the human person, they had founded a theological center with the pope's blessing called the Pontifical John Paul II Institute for Studies on Marriage and Family. Albacete began teaching there occasionally. Eventually plans were drawn up to open a branch of the Institute in Boston, and, in 1985, he and his mother and brother moved there. The visionary plan collapsed, however, when the promised funding for the center suddenly dried up. Fr. Lorenzo was deeply disappointed, but by then he was dealing with a far worse calamity.

"A few days after my arrival in Boston, my mother began her ten year purgatory as a victim of Alzheimer's disease," Albacete later explained in a letter to Fr. Luigi Giussani, an Italian priest who had founded the Catholic lay movement Communion and Liberation. "One year after our arrival in Boston, she had to be placed in a nursing home after eight months in the hospital." The inexorable physical and mental deterioration of his mother deeply affected Albacete. He recorded his anguish in a poem:

> What do you remember
> When you look at me?
> Where are you watching me from?
> Where have you gone, mother?
> What has happened to everything you wanted?
> Do you no longer want it?
> Do you no longer care?
> Your motherly soul,
> what moves it?

"The economic effects on my life were devastating," Albacete later explained to Fr. Giussani. "With now two mentally ill persons entirely under my care, my daily schedule was destroyed." For the next two years, Albacete's days were completely packed with visits to St. Elizabeth's Hospital where his mother was a patient, while trying to look after Manuel, who was also deeply distraught by their mother's illness and who would keep his brother up at all hours with worries and questions. Then there were the futile attempts to keep the Institute project afloat, not to mention all his regular priestly duties, which he faithfully carried out in two parishes near the hospital.

The stress affected Albacete physically, psychologically, and spiritually. There were dark moments when he felt abandoned by God. His weight increased dramatically during his Boston years. "I think I have a lot of anger," he wrote during this time. "My mind runs and runs." Yet even in the worst of his trials, Albacete kept his sense of humor and still treasured the everyday wonders and simple joys that life offered—a Broadway song on the radio, bull sessions with friends as he chain-smoked, shopping for a new fountain pen, or reminiscing with Manuel, who possessed an astonishing memory. At the core of his consciousness, however, was his awareness of "the intimate—mystical—relationship between Christ and the believer." Simply put, it was his friendship with the Mystery made man, God present among us, that made it possible for him to live a truly human life, even under seemingly impossible circumstances.

Years later, a parishioner who attended one of the churches Albacete served recalled the impact of his "guileless, angelic countenance" while he was preaching.

†

Early on in his priesthood, Fr. Lorenzo had met a businessman named William Carrigan who had encountered Padre Pio of Pietrelcina while serving in Italy during World War II. "In him we have found the true opposite of hate," Carrigan told friends back in the States. "And in the violence of this war, contact with the Love of Christ through this favored Priest is a shock to our thinking."

Carrigan devoted the rest of his life to making Padre Pio's story known, a devotion that increased after his wife underwent a mortal illness. Their shared experience of suffering drew Carrigan and Albacete together in a mutual desire to understand how the poor and sick might be more adequately served by their caregivers.

In May 1990, at Carrigan's urging, Albacete went to San Giovanni Rotondo, the commune in Foggia, Italy, where Padre Pio had established a hospital and research center alongside churches and an ancient monastery. The notes he scribbled down during his visit mingled observation and prayer:

> So, here I am, Lord. You alone are Lord. You conquered sin and death through your sufferings and resurrection. It's suffering that brings me here. You know it is. It is because of my mother's sufferings, what it has cost to relieve them, how I want to be the priest of the meaning behind her suffering. So I am here at the place of the House for the Relief of Suffering.

He toured the medical facilities over the next two days, noting the mobs of tourists outside the hospital, a sign of "popular piety in all its glory." He reflected on what Padre Pio thought when he saw them. "People are here expressing a need," Albacete concluded. "They are here because they suffer." The visit to the hospital and, in particular, with the nuns who worked as nurses there, left Albacete deeply impressed, but also full of even more questions:

> Suppose my mother was in that hospital, would I experience the involvement of God more than at St. Elizabeth's by looking outside and not seeing Boston (the world of human pretention) but the world of human need gathering because God acted here in the life of Padre Pio?

By this time, Lorenzo Albacete had moved back to Washington, DC. He was now a monsignor. Another attempt had been made to bring the John Paul II Institute to the US, this time to the nation's capital. In agreeing to the plan, the Holy Father requested that Albacete be hired by the Institute as a lecturer and made its Director of Studies. It meant another difficult move for his family, of course, but at least they would all be in a more stable situation. Before Conchita Albacete could be moved to a nursing home, she first had an extended stay at Providence Hospital, where she was treated for a skin ulcer. Albacete and Carrigan began to meet with doctors and nurses there to speak about Padre Pio's example and engage in a dialogue about the meaning of their work. A Padre Pio prayer group was established at the hospital, and Albacete celebrated Mass at their monthly meetings.

Monsignor Albacete had much to pray over and ponder—beginning with his sense of powerlessness in the face of the sufferings of his mother and brother. His visit to San Giovanni Rotondo and all that ensued from it had helped him see the situation in a new, more mature light. Always an avid reader, he was increasingly drawn to certain Catholic novelists, like Flannery O'Connor and Walker Percy, who had grappled with many of the same questions. In addition to these writers, there was his study of John Paul II's Christocentric theology and its ramifications for the person, particularly the downtrodden and those who suffered. This rich tapestry of experiences and influences formed the basis of a series of lectures that were presented at Providence Hospital to healthcare professionals from around the country as well as members of the public. Co-sponsored by the John Paul II Institute, the five-lecture series was titled "The Relief of Suffering." This book is drawn from that material, in a slightly edited form.

†

The years that followed Albacete's "The Relief of Suffering" lectures would prove to be a living out of his assertion that life is a dramatic dialogue that "points towards the origin of this drama, to the author, to a script not written by us, and not written on earth." Through his involvement with the John Paul II Institute, Albacete became friends with Angelo Scola, a fellow priest who sometimes taught courses at the Institute and who would go on to become the Patriarch of Venice and the Archbishop of Milan. "There was something about him that I had never seen in a priest," Albacete later recounted. He found himself drawn towards Scola's freedom in front of reality and his openness to "everything that was good (and) interesting."

Whenever Albacete would inquire about how he "was the way he was," Scola would say it was because he had been educated by Fr. Luigi Giussani, the founder of Communion and Liberation (CL). The answer made Albacete even more curious. He peppered Scola with questions until finally an exasperated Scola arranged a meeting with Giussani in Milan in 1993. During their lunch, Giussani asked Albacete to help the CL movement become rooted in America. It was the beginning of a personal friendship and an involvement with the movement that would slowly develop and blossom over the next twenty years.

In 1995, the moment that Lorenzo had been most dreading came to pass when Conchita Albacete died at a nursing home in Washington run by the Little Sisters of the Poor. Though his mother had been unable to speak or acknowledge anyone for years, Lorenzo visited her regularly, speaking to her as if she could understand him and celebrating the Eucharist for the staff and patients. In the funeral homily, Monsignor Albacete confessed that "each time I celebrated Mass in this chapel, or even walked through it, each time I walked past the viewing room, I felt a chill in my heart and knew someday I would have a terrifying date to keep in this place." He regarded his mother's death as a moment of passage that tested his faith. "Suddenly she has become one with that Other Presence, and my way to her is clearly now only through Him. She has become the challenge, the claim, the question: 'I am the Resurrection and the Life....Do you believe this?'"

Just a few months after his mother's death, Pope John Paul II informed Albacete that he intended to appoint him to the presidency of the Pontifical Catholic University of Puerto Rico. Albacete was hesitant to accept but was persuaded when the Pope insisted that he needed Albacete's help as the Third Millennium approached, explaining his desire to build a bridge between the churches in Puerto Rico and New York City. Under Albacete's leadership, the university in Ponce could be transformed into a respected institution of higher learning where Hispanic heritage and culture could encounter and engage in dialogue with academics and professionals from all over the island, the mainland US, and around the world. The vision was expansive and exciting—but first Albacete would have to convince his brother Manuel to move back to Puerto Rico.

Manuel Albacete's illness had worsened. Leaving the house had always been an anxiety-inducing challenge for him, but by the time of the proposed Puerto Rico move, Manuel had become a recluse. His emotional outbursts and often outrageous demands had also worsened. As a rule, he refused to ride in an elevator or in an airplane, except under the most extraordinary circumstances. Getting Manuel to agree to the Puerto Rico relocation took all of Lorenzo's ingenuity. In the end, he used Manuel's obsession with spotted cows to entice him to move. Purchasing a number of small stuffed animal cows, Albacete had them lined up in specific locations along their itinerary, including a long line of cows that led into their new home in Ponce. The tactic delighted Manuel, and soon the Albacete brothers were settled in their new home.

Lorenzo Albacete immediately set to work rewriting the university curriculum, addressing the faculty and students, putting together a group of outside advisors, and meeting with donors to raise the funds needed to carry out his agenda. Within months of Albacete's appointment, however, some board members contrived with bishops from the island to have him ousted. Their reasons were strictly political. Before he had even taken office, the pope had warned Albacete that the bishops in Puerto Rico were "afraid and jealous" of him. They were greatly displeased when the Holy Father rejected their own nominee to make Albacete president—and the sense of resentment only deepened when Albacete's intellect and humor made him a center of attention on the island.

Albacete's tenure ended abruptly. The results of a university audit that he had himself ordered were turned against Albacete in order to accuse him of mismanagement. His supporters advised him to fight back and see his mission through. Close friends feared that the ouster would permanently injure his reputation—as it did to an extent. One of them urged Albacete to "directly confront the charge" and to leak the complete results of the audit to the press. Albacete, unwilling to cause a scandal that might harm the Church, did not heed the advice.

Expecting to return to Washington, Albacete was taken aback when his superior Cardinal Hickey informed him otherwise. When the Archbishop of New York John Cardinal O'Connor learned of Albacete's situation, he requested that Albacete be sent to teach at the archdiocesan seminary in Yonkers, New York. Like John Paul II, O'Connor believed it was crucial for the Church to actively engage contemporary culture. He had long admired Albacete's intellect and ability to communicate the faith. "You could be our new Chesterton," he told Albacete, "but for that, you have to be here." Albacete gratefully accepted O'Connor's invitation but remained shaken by his failure in Puerto Rico. "I felt totally lost," he explained to Giussani. "I had no resources, very little energy, and I could not understand what was happening."

Lorenzo was also grateful for the presence of the CL community in New York City. He felt accepted and embraced by its members. "It seemed that the Lord had rejected all of my initiatives," he told Fr. Giussani. "And indeed He had, in order to bring me finally to the place and the context where I would learn to obey Him first. The movement in New York received me with a love and enthusiasm that made me recognize this."

The relocation to New York City would prove to be fruitful for Albacete and the Church. As Cardinal O'Connor had hoped, it marked a period of close involvement with the media and culture at large. Albacete struck up close friendships with figures like Hendrik Hertzberg, the executive editor of *The New Yorker*, and Helen Whitney, a producer and documentarian who made films for PBS. Unfortunately, O'Connor died of brain cancer before he could see his generosity bear fruit. As Albacete recounted:

> A little before Cardinal O'Connor died he told me that he was sorry not to be here and see what would happen to "what we have begun here," and that he should have acted sooner. Still, he said, "If I go to heaven I will help you from there." And indeed, the day he died I received my offer to write a column for *The New York Times*."

Over a ten year period, Albacete's writings appeared in the pages of the New York Times Magazine, The New Yorker, The New York Daily News, and the Milanese newspaper Tempi, among others. His book God at the Ritz earned critical praise, and he became a regular guest on CNN and The Charlie Rose Show. In collaboration with Helen Whitney, Albacete appeared on episodes of the PBS series Frontline confronting issues ranging from the legacy of Pope John Paul II to the role that religious belief played in the tragedy of 9/11. When an important event or crisis arose, Albacete became a "go-to" media voice for the Church who was sure to answer questions with frankness, intelligence, and wit. He also spoke at conferences on science and faith and debated the atheist writer Christopher Hitchens at New York's Pierre Hotel. In Helen Whitney's words, Albacete became "a brilliant missionary to the secular world." All these activities were in addition to the speaking engagements, retreats, and travels on behalf of Communion and Liberation.

It was an exhausting schedule, one made more stressful by his responsibility for his brother. Returning to his home in Yonkers, Lorenzo would find Manuel waiting up for him, wanting to talk through the night. Often when he had to get some work done or needed to make a call, Manuel would insist that Lorenzo reminisce about the past, help put together a weather chart (one of Manuel's obsessions), or answer some of the endless questions that sprang from his hyperactive mind. There were darker moments, too, filled with accusations and resentments, that grew harsher as Manuel's illness worsened. Even on trips, Albacete would spend much of his time on a cell phone trying to pacify his brother. There were lighter moments, of course, when a funny story would send them both into fits of laughter, or when they would celebrate a small triumph together.

"Monsignor's life was a roller coaster," according to Olivetta Danese, a member of CL who managed Albacete's schedule for eighteen years. At the suggestion of Fr. Giussani, Albacete became the reference point for the house of Memores Domini (a lay association within Communion and Liberation consecrated to virginity), where Danese lived with other women. Visiting the house became a regular part of Albacete's routine. Those years were marked by the knowledge that he was using his gifts in service of the Gospel, had found a home in the CL movement, and was surrounded by friends who loved him—but none of these things could alleviate his intense spiritual suffering—his feelings of inner desolation and sometimes a sense of having been abandoned by God. In reality, the struggles that Albacete recorded in his diaries in the 1970s and 80s remained throughout his life. Quietly, unknown to most people who knew him for his jokes and larger-than-life personality, Albacete was engaged in an intense, continuous, and often excruciating dialogue with the same "Mystery" that he spoke of in his talks. His own suffering, and in particular his shared ordeals with Manuel, made up much of the substance of this dialogue, his own sharing in Christ's passion.

Some outsiders believed that Albacete's relationship with his brother created a "missed opportunity," a burden that prevented Lorenzo Albacete from living out his vocation and evangelical mission to their fullest extent. Viewed in this way, Monsignor Albacete's life was defined by a tragedy—a sad story dominated by a younger brother who was the victim of a mental illness that devastated the lives of both Albacete brothers. Christopher West, a student of Albacete's at the John Paul II Institute, sees the situation differently:

> Monsignor could have had a theological career that was more in the limelight, but he sacrificed that to live what he believed in loving his brother. He was misunderstood and even criticized and persecuted for doing so—and I say more power to you, Monsignor, for living what you knew to be true. The fruit for the Body of Christ is far more potent in the love that Monsignor showed his brother than any fruit he could have borne for the Church in writing more books or being more "fruitful" as a theologian.

As tempting as it might be to try to synthesize Albacete's spirituality into a "way" of living Christianity that others might imitate, it would do no justice to the man or his faith. Albacete did not live a "way," but a relationship. He was unapologetically himself before other people and before God, with all his intelligence at play, his desire, sins, humor, earthly interests, capacity and incapacity for love and mercy, and his sufferings big and small. In trusting himself to the Mystery as it appeared to him through his relationship with his brother and others, in the sacramental life of the Church, in prayer and offering—and even in fountain pens and Broadway musicals—he experienced a familiarity with this Mystery that verged on the mystical, though, like the man himself, his mysticism was utterly distinctive in character. A few stories may serve as a small window into this relatively overlooked aspect of Albacete's life and witness.

There was the time, for instance, when he was driving across Puerto Rico with Olivetta Danese on the way to a public event. Passing a beggar on the road, Monsignor Albacete suddenly braked the car and gave all the money in his wallet to the destitute man on the roadside. As Albacete drove off, Olivetta chided him.

> "I can understand giving alms," I said, "but you have no money! You know how hard it is to pay any of your bills. Why did you give all your money away?" And he looked at me with a kind of pity, and he said, "You don't understand. One day when I am in front of God, and I show my empty hands, that man will be there to say a good word for me." This is the way Monsignor would survive. This *was* his faith, his relationship with God.

Young people often sought out Albacete when they were going through difficulties, because he spoke to them as equals, offering not advice, but the authentic friendship of one who had been changed by the encounter with Jesus. Once a woman named Rita was agonized by a vocational crisis. She told Albacete that she was afraid of going against what Christ wanted for her life. "Monsignor was very emphatic," Rita remembered. "He said to me, 'Don't you understand? Christ will never let go of you. He can't! He can't!'" And when Albacete taught at the seminary, he befriended Louis, one of the seminarians who was having a difficult experience there. Albacete would take Louis to a nearby diner and listen to him complain over cheeseburgers. "I remember one time I was just cursing and swearing, I think I was hitting the table. And he would just sit there smoking, saying, 'Yes, yes.'" Albacete later mused: "Think about what would happen if a king or royalty came to visit your house. You have somebody great there, but your house is a mess. The living room is wrecked. There are a thousand people around, it's chaos!" Albacete understood from his own experience how disruption and disarray could often be a sign of God's presence.

In the summer of 2009, Lorenzo Albacete's physical and mental strength began to weaken. The demands of making public appearances and of traveling, along with the strain of caring for Manuel, were proving too much for him. In July, while meeting with the women of the Memores Domini house, he told them that in the past months a question had dominated his thoughts:

> What did Fr. Giussani see in me? How to explain the confidence that he seemed to have in me from the first day until the last one in which Olivetta was present? That disturbed me because [Giussani] could see that I could not understand him in a good way. I did understand him theoretically, but I did not understand him in experience. I began to say that maybe he saw that the day will come when I will be forced to confront this and then I thought that the day has come ... and then came my discovery that I was not able to take trips anymore because of the care of my brother, then my complete breakdown about one month ago when I was not even able to leave my house. At that moment I realized that the time had arrived to surrender my intellectual abilities and ask for help, which I think He is responding to right now. In any case, since that moment and during these past three weeks I realized... that every day I have to offer my nothingness until the last attachment to my ideas is

cut off. I'm now free, there is an emptiness. St. Paul
uses the word for Christ. He self-emptied. This self-
emptiness is amazing because it's not pleasant but
it's joyful; it can even coincide with an emotional
fear. Eventually along the path you start to see
things differently, you see changes everywhere.

Lorenzo began to evince the symptoms of
Parkinson's disease, the same illness that had taken the
lives of John Paul II and Luigi Giussani, the two men
who had so shaped the course of his life and vocation.
The diagnosis was later confirmed by a neurologist.
Medications helped reduce his shaking, but the side
effects proved to be nearly as debilitating as the disease
itself. Even short trips were now an ordeal. When he made
an occasional public appearance, Lorenzo's mind was
still sharp and his passion was as evident as ever, but his
ability to communicate became severely impeded. As he
sensed the end approaching, Albacete became increasingly
worried about what would become of Manuel when he
was gone. He asked Christopher West to look after his
brother, which West faithfully did until Manuel's own
death in 2022.

In February 2014, Lorenzo Albacete was admitted to
the hospital, but, as the months passed, it was clear that
there was little doctors could do for him. He was placed
in a nursing home in October, where he received a stream
of visitors. Among them was Vince, a college student who
came to visit Monsignor Albacete with another friend, Gil.
The date was October 23. These would be the last hours
of Albacete's life. Vince wrote in his diary about how
Albacete introduced them to the nurse as "my students,
indirectly." Half an hour later, a chaplain arrived with the

Blessed Sacrament. Albacete received communion. "After bowing his head for a moment, he looked up distantly and said clearly, 'Jesus always comes. He always wants to be with us.'"

Vince remembered how he and Gil took turns holding Albacete's hand as they told Albacete about their studies. When Gil told him that he was a philosophy student, Albacete perked up and explained how the Communion and Liberation movement had had to contend with the Marxism that dominated Italian society in the 1950s and 60s:

> "What is there like that in our country now?" he asked Gil. Gil answered: "It is my friendship with my friends at school that allows me to see the world clearly." Monsignor looked at him, joy in his eyes and smiling. "Isn't it beautiful?" he said, holding Gil's hand tightly.
>
> He then became very serious and told us that nights are the hardest for him. "People are passing by, and nobody ever stops. I am so alone at night. Last night I was screaming, and no one stopped." It was the hardest part of being at the nursing home for him, because, as his biological clock had been screwy for a long time, he was often awake at night, confined to the bed and alone. "Will you stay with me tonight?" he asked us, pleadingly. "Will you stay with me?" Gil immediately said that we would. "Go and ask them, make sure you can stay," he said. "You don't know how much this means to me. This will be a great service to me and to the Church."

That evening Albacete slept peacefully, while the two young men did their best to keep watch through the night. Eventually, they also drifted off to sleep, and, when

Vince awoke at around seven a.m., there were nurses in the room:

> I saw the oxygen tube trailing off the bed and looked at him. He was not moving and looked so pale. Then one of the nurses placed her hands on his eyelids and pressed them down, and I jolted upwards. I sat up, scared. "What's going on?" The nurse looked back at me. "I'm sorry," she said. "He passed." I ran to the bed and grabbed his hand, staring into his face. "Eternal rest grant unto him, O Lord, and let perpetual light shine upon him." The prayer came to my lips, although all I felt was a hollow shock.

It was a Friday, the day of the Passion, when Lorenzo Albacete went to the Lord to show his empty hands.

Acknowledgments

THE ALBACETE FORUM WOULD like to thank Somos Community Care for the generous support that made the publication of this book possible.

We are also grateful to Gregory and Suzanne M. Wolfe for their meticulous and sensitive editing of Lorenzo Albacete's original lectures into their present form in this book. The commitment and passion that Slant Books has shown in bringing Lorenzo Albacete's works into print are truly exemplary.

Special thanks to Lisa Lickona who provided valuable feedback for this book. She and Mary Beth Newkumet also conducted interviews for the biographical chapter. We extend our gratitude to the following individuals who agreed to be interviewed: Olivetta Danese, Fr. Francis Early, Louis Giovino, Angelo Matera, Rita Simmonds, and Christopher West. We are also indebted to Vince Petruccelli for allowing us to use excerpts from his diary about the last night of Lorenzo Albacete's life.

There are many other people whom Lorenzo Albacete would have wanted to thank were he still with us. But surely, as he did in his first book *God at the Ritz*, Lorenzo would have ended by saying:

Y *gracias especiales a tí*, Manuel.

The Albacete Forum was founded in 2017 to preserve and promote the legacy and works of Lorenzo Albacete. The materials that formed the basis of this book, along with the Albacete materials quoted in the short biography, were collected and archived by the Forum. More information about The Albacete Forum's mission and activities can be found at their website, www.albaceteforum.org.

This book was set in Rialto dF, designed
by Giovanni de Faccio and Lui Karner from CAST—
Cooperativa Anonima Servizi Tipografici. Rialto dF
is a book face inspired by calligraphic tradition. Named
after the famous bridge in Venice, it was conceived as
a bridge between calligraphy and typography, roman
and italic.

This book was designed by Shannon Carter,
Ian Creeger, and Gregory Wolfe. It was published
in hardcover, paperback, and electronic formats
by Slant Books, Seattle, Washington.

Cover photograph: Getty Images.

Lightning Source UK Ltd.
Milton Keynes UK
UKHW012046060223
416584UK00007B/235

9 781639 821266